The Big Book of
Cards & Toasts For Almost
All Occasions
Express Yourself in Rhyme

Marcia Goldlist

ISBN-10: 1482334828
ISBN-13: 978-1482334821

DEDICATION

This book is dedicated to all those who love to celebrate life.

CONTENTS

INTRODUCTION

This book is the complete selection
Of three books which I put into one collection.
Birthday Cards & Toasts, *Cards & Toasts For Almost All Occasions* and
Cards, Toasts & Notes For the Office I took
And put them all into this book.
For cards and toasts you really won't have to worry about creating a
delight,
As you have so many choices in this book that one is sure to be just
right.
With this book it is easy to get across your message in just the right
way
As you have so much choice that for almost any situation you will
find something to say.
But you can always take some lines from one rhyme and some from
another
And end up with just the right poem for your friend, colleague,
cousin, mother or brother.
With this book, no matter what the situation, you will find that it is
not hard
To write the perfect card!

.

ANNIVERSARY

~Anniversary -1

Congratulations on your anniversary!
It is clear that your love is not cursory.
*20 years together is really neat,
Especially today it is quite a feat.
May your love only increase.
May your friendship never cease.
Tonight you both deserve a drink,
And over all of your accomplishments you should rethink.
You both deserve to smile,
For together you have accomplished much that is worthwhile.
May your marriage continue with zest.
May your years together be blessed.

*Change to the appropriate number.

~Anniversary -2

May your love only increase.
May your friendship never cease.
You both deserve to smile,
For together you have accomplished much that is worthwhile.
Wishing you together good health and happy times galore.
No matter what don't lose that spark in each other that you adore!
May your marriage continue with zest.
May your remaining years be blessed.

~Anniversary -3

Today is certainly an important day,
Worth celebrating in a special way.
Celebrate your love as husband and wife
And work together to make sure that you each get the most out of
life.

~Anniversary -4

To *Bill and Jill we would like to raise our glasses,
As **40 years together does not come to the masses.
Hard times we are sure that you went through,
But we hope that looking back there were only a few.
And so it requires a number of cheers,
Because you worked through your differences for **40 years.
We wish for you that you continue to get along,
And that you help each other to be strong.
Of course health is important too,
So we hope that this is something that accompanies both of you.
We hope that lots more laughs you will share,
And that each of you is always aware that the other one for you does
care.
May you enjoy family and friends at many celebrations,
And tranquility and adventure on vacations.
In short, you should continue to enjoy life,
As husband and wife.

*Change to the appropriate names.
**Change to the appropriate number.

~Anniversary -5

So, together you've been for *25 years,
And you're still happy it appears.
Well you've beaten the odds and that's just great,
Because over your love for each other we want no debate.
We wish you many more happy years together,
Smiling and **taking pictures in all kinds of weather.
Much pride and joy may your kids bring to you,
And together as a family many great memories may you accrue.

*Change to the appropriate number.
**Fill in something that the couple likes to do together (travelling,
playing tennis, working together, etc.)

~Anniversary -6

So you think that your anniversary slipped our mind,
But we simply decided to have a celebration of a different kind.
So enjoy being pampered like a queen and king,
Because this just may be the last time that for you we do such a thing.

~Anniversary -7

Wow!! You've been together for *thirty-six years,
With lots to celebrate and we hope not too many tears.
**You have already lived together for the years equaling double *chai*,
That your lives have been blessed twice, this does imply.
Just think of over how many flowers,
And how many dinners you've spent hours.
More importantly perhaps is the amount of time together that you
have simply enjoyed.
Hopefully there has not been much that you have felt that you had to
avoid.
You have helped each other become who you each are,
So look at your handiwork and see in the other your own personal
star.
It doesn't really matter what you have amassed,
Marriage is about the times that you were there for each other in the
past,
And knowing that in the future the other will be there,
With advice, love, support and a prayer.

*You may change the number if you take out lines three and four.
**If you don't know what this means don't worry just take out lines
three and four.

~Anniversary -8

To a special couple that has been married for *30 years,
We raise our glasses and offer cheers!
You made it clear from the beginning that there were things that you
both wanted to achieve,
So in your own quiet way you found a lifestyle in which you did
believe.
It is now *30 years later,
And to your values neither of you has been a traitor.
**Together you have raised two girls and a boy.
To the family and so many more you have brought joy.
***Jill and ***Bill your marriage really is an inspiration.
Now relax for a bit and go together on a vacation!

*Fill in the number of years.
**You can of course change the number of girls or take them out. If
there are no boys or there is more than one, just leave out the two
corresponding lines.
***Change to the appropriate names.

~Anniversary -9

Today is your anniversary day
And we hope that it is special in at least a little way.
*This is anniversary number one
And we hope that this is just the beginning of lots of fun.
Truth be told marriage can be hard,
But it certainly is not something that you should discard.
It takes work and love and patience too.
That is the way a marriage you should pursue.
Keep showing each other that you care
And your dreams and fears share.
Together you can go a long way
So help each other be strong every day!

*To use this poem for a different anniversary year take out lines three
and four.

~Anniversary -10

We hope that tonight will add,
To the memories that you already had,
Of this special time in your life,
Which we hope is passing without any strife.
Know that we are thinking of you,
Hoping that your life will be blessed through and through.

BIRTH

Many of the poems in this section can be altered slightly and used as congratulations for grandparents. Likewise some of the poems in the grandparents section can be changed slightly and used for parents.

~Birth -1

Congratulations on this great event.
A *child is a very special present.
Enjoy all the simple moments as **she grows up,
Like **her learning how to crawl or drink from a cup.
Congratulations from us all.
If you need any advice feel free on us to call.

*Can write son or daughter.
**Change for masculine.

~Birth -2

Welcome to this world,
Into which you were hurled.
It is not always the greatest place,
But there are many things worthy of your embrace.
And anyone; young or old,
Can make good things unfold.
A simple smile,
Can help others get over a trial.
May your goodness spread.
May you never be without enough bread.
May you always be healthy,
And consider yourself wealthy.
May you always find things to be in awe of,
And may you always feel surrounded by love.

~Birth -3

Congratulations on becoming a parent for the first time.
We know that this is something in your life that is prime.

~Birth -4

Coming into this world may not have been your choice,
But we want you to know that for your birth we do rejoice.
May you have a full life,
Without too much strife.
May you be blessed with self-pride,
And eventually *with a wonderful bride.
May you be well in body and mind,
And to the wonders in nature may you never be blind.
May you always feel surrounded by love,
And that there are things to feel in awe of.
May you learn the wonders of a smile,
And feel free to say "I love you" once in a while.

*For a girl substitute "be" for "with"

~Birth -5

Congratulations on your *daughter, who is still quite new.
May *she grow up with the values that you imbue.
We wish for *her health,
And a moderate amount of wealth.
We hope that with *her you will dance and sing,
And some day you will share the joy with *her when **she receives a
wedding ring.
Enjoy with *her each and every quiet time.
They can really be sublime.
Right now *she is small,
But before you can turn around *she will be tall.
So kiss and hug *her now,
While *she will still allow.
Enjoy each and every smile.
We know that you'll make your time together worthwhile.
Congratulations once again,
And to all of *her prayers we say amen.

*You can change daughter to son. In this case change she to he, her
to him and "she receives" to "he gives".

Grandchild

Many of the poems in this section can be changed slightly and used for the parents. Likewise check out the above birth section for poems which can be modified for grandparents.

~Grandchild -1

A baby is on its way,
And I probably won't be here for that special day.
I hope that all goes well,
And that you enjoy that new baby smell.
Each grandchild is special in his or her own way.
Have fun discovering how this one changes while for even a few days
you are away.

~Grandchild -2

We're so happy that things went well.
Now you have a *granddaughter and we think that that is swell!
May you have many good times together as *she grows up.
Enjoy all the simple things like *her learning to drink from a cup.
May *she always know good health,
And understand that there are more important things than wealth.
May *she value having family nearby,
And lots of pride may *she to you supply.
Congratulations from us all,
And don't forget to let us know when *she begins to crawl!

*Can be changed to grandson. In this case change she to he, and her to him.

~Grandchild -3

This is to let you know,
That we are thinking of you today as your family by one does grow.

You've waited patiently for this day,
And now it has come and the baby is on his way.

Actually, the doctor will take him or her out,
But even if about coming out he still has a doubt,
He will soon know what love is really about.

~Grandchild -4

Congratulations on this great event!
A *granddaughter is a very special present.
May health and happiness be given to you both,
And may you have much pride as you watch *her in her growth.
May you have many special times with your *granddaughter in the years ahead,
And may you be honoured to see *her wed.

*Can be changed to the masculine.

Grandparent's Announcement of a Grandson

*We are in awe,
For now *we are Grandpa and Grandma.
**My little girl gave birth to a healthy boy,
And the whole family is filled with joy.

*May substitute *"I am" in first line and "I am a Grandma" in second line.
**Can be changed to "My little boy now has his own healthy boy."

Congratulations for a New Grandson

~Grandson -1

Congratulations!
You have just added one more to the number of your relations.
We are so glad that all is well,
And we hope that you will only have happy things to tell.
May you have much pride from your new grandson.
With him may you have a lot of fun.
Enjoy watching him grow,
May love between you flow.

~Grandson -2

Congratulations on your new grandson.
Happier for you we could be none.
*And he lives right next door,
So with him you can develop a great rapport.
May the two of you spend many special times together,
In all sorts of weather.
With him we are sure you will have lots of fun,
Playing, and walking with him out in the sun.
*And now that you have lots more room,
Even if it rains you can play things like putting on a costume.
We're sure that he will delight you for hours at a time,
And you will have many moments together that are sublime.
May health and happiness be given to you both,
And may you have much pride as you watch him in his growth.

*Take out these two corresponding lines if they are not relevant.

~Grandson -3

Congratulations on your first grandson.
A new stage in your lives has just begun.
What names will you go by now?
*Grandpa and Grandma or Nana and Gramps will you allow?
Photo albums by the dozen you will now have to acquire,
As pictures by the hundreds you will desire.
May you have much pride as you watch him grow to become a man,
And have quality time when he comes and asks you for help when he makes a plan.
May you have many special times with your grandson in the years ahead,
And may you be honoured to see him wed.

*You can change the names given.

~Grandson -4

You must feel relieved…and grateful…and excited
And anxious to be united.
Now you'll really be busy with *two little boys,
Both wanting your attention and making all sorts of noise.
But you are sure to feel just great,
As you can go home and relax before making another play date.

*You may change the number.

BIRTHDAY WISHES

Age Specific

Age 1

We hope that you are happy to be one!
And that you find life lots of fun!!
Your kisses and hugs we love to feel.
We all love you a great deal!

Age 2

A clown might be funny,
But you are our hunny bunny!
We are so excited that you are now two,
But most of all we want to tell you that we love you!

Age 3

It's hard to believe that you are already three
And learning your ABC's.
You are really very sweet
And being with you is a treat.

Age 4

Now that you're four
We want to see you more and more.
To be with you is so much fun,
That we don't want our time together to be done.

Age 5

You sure are special to me.
With you I love to be.
I love when together we play
Happy 5th birthday!

Bar/Bat Mitzvah

~Bar/Bat Mitzvah -1

With your skills we were impressed,
And it was nice to be counted among your guests.
May doing *mitzvot* bring you joy,
Much thoughtfulness may you employ.
We hope that you will always be a proud Jew,
And that being a good Jew is something that you will pursue.

~Bar/Bat Mitzvah -2

On becoming a *Bat Mitzvah we want to congratulate you.
From now on *mitzvot* are your responsibility to pursue.
For helping others your parents are both known,
But it is now up to you, for your life to set the tone.
We're sure that you will choose well,
And that you will excel.
May your choices be for the best
And may you always be blessed.

*Can substitute Bar.

~Bar/Bat Mitzvah -3

Mazel Tov to you!
It was great to see you in your debut
As a full-fledged Jew!

In reading from the Torah you did excel,
Your speech went well,
And your party was swell!

Now as a responsible Jew your life does start,
So take it to heart!

Let your Judaism be a guide
In things that you need to decide.

Being Jewish is not something to hide
It is something in which you should feel pride!

~Bar/Bat Mitzvah -4

As a *Bar Mitzvah you're off to a great start!
We're so proud that of the Jewish people you are a part.

*Can substitute Bat.

To the Parents of the Bar Mitzvah Boy

~Parents-1

I'm sure that you remember kissing your little baby.
While, now *he is about to be called to the Torah and you get to
kiss *him maybe.
Time has passed.
It moves very fast.
So slow down and enjoy the time that *he lets you spend together.
Enjoy your walks and talks in all kinds of weather.
Soon, *he'll be out of the house,
Living with *his spouse.
But *he is at home now,
And you're doing a great job with *him so take a bow.
*Although the hard work is not yet done,
Enjoy the achievements of your son.

*For a girl change masculine to feminine and remove the last two
lines. If being called to the Torah is not appropriate for the girl just
remove "he is about to be called to the Torah and".

~Parents -2

We hope that everything on the weekend goes well,
And that the whole celebration is really swell.
May you have much pride from your son,
Even though as a teenager the fun has just begun!

20 Years Old

It is hard to believe that you are turning twenty,
On the other hand your accomplishments are already many.
You have already created your own path in life,
And you seemed to do it without any strife.
We are very proud of you,
And we wish you success in anything you decide to pursue.

22 Years Old

We want to wish you a very happy birthday,
With the hope that this year will be special in every way.
You are now twenty-two,
And we are not quite sure where the time flew.
May you be blessed with health,
And knowing that the most important thing in life is not wealth.

Birthdays Ending in 3
*Can be changed to any age ending in a 3 beginning at 23.

~Birthdays Ending in 3 -1

Your birthday is coming up soon,
So we would like to celebrate with you this afternoon.
This year you are turning *63,
And that it should be a special year for you we all agree.
We hope that this year you will begin to start taking better care of
yourself,
Because some things should just not be put on the shelf.
We hope that you enjoy this coming year,
And that you know that our wishes are sincere.

~Birthdays Ending in 3 -2

With the age of *53,
You seem to agree.
Just keep enjoying this day all year long,
Remembering not too much is so bad that it can't be overcome by
thinking of all the good in your life and singing a song.

30 Years Old

Wow! You are now thirty,
And you still seem pretty sturdy.
May your love for *Bill grow,
And your discoveries flow.
May your health be good,
And you feel understood.
May you have a great year,
And your worries disappear.

*You can write the name of a spouse, or special friend, or something that the person likes to do.

40 Years Old

So, this year you turned the big four oh,
And we hope that to you this isn't a big blow.
Just keep enjoying your time with your kids and *your wife,
Because that's what is important in life.
Pamper yourself, 'cause that is key,
Make sure that for yourself some time is free.
May your work give you much satisfaction,
And with your co-workers may you enjoy the interaction!
We all wish you a successful year,
May it be one that brings you lots of cheer!

*For a wife you can write, "and as XXX's wife."

45 Years Old

Congratulations to our *man who is turning forty-five,
It is a wonder that with us you have survived!
This gift is just a little display,
Of our love for you on your birthday!

*Can be changed to gal.

50 Years Old

~50 Years Old -1

This year 50 you are turning,
And you realize that life is about more than just what you are earning.
Family is of prime importance to you,
And family get-togethers you do pursue.
We appreciate your caring
And all of your sharing.
Today we want to take the opportunity to thank you
For all that you do!
Here's a toast to you and your special day.
May this year be good to you in every way!

~50 Years Old -2

50 you are turning this year
And perhaps you approach this with a bit of fear.
Well, don't be worried
And don't feel hurried.
You're just reaching your prime,
And we hope that in health you will live a long time!
The hardest part of your work is done,
Now go out and have some fun!

55 Years Old

~55 Years Old -1

Congratulations on turning fifty-five,
And being very much alive!
I know that you don't really want to be reminded of your age,
But you've already done so much that by you we set our gauge.
May this year be filled with many things that get you to smile,
And many moments that you deem worthwhile.
We wish for you a healthy and satisfying year,
With good friends near.
Don't worry about the number of candles on your cake,
Or even any minor ache.
Remember that life is all about what you do when you are awake,
And we are sure that you will stay young with all that you partake!

~55 Years Old -2

Happy Birthday to you,
We hope that all year you never feel blue.
Now that you are fifty-five,
We hope that you will survive
Cause we don't know what we would do without you.
Our love for you is always true!

60 Years Old

~60 Years Old -1

So you are turning 60 years old!
It is a great age we are told.
If you don't want to do something just say, "Oy, I am so old",
Yet you are still young enough to have many adventures unfold.
You have 60 more years until you reach 120,
So good times and joy you can still have plenty.
We know that you have done many things of which you can be proud,
And that you are a great friend we will all declare out loud.
Make the best out of the rest of your life.
Try to keep a low level to your strife.
Enjoy your friends,
When the need arises make amends.
Wisely use your time,
Because all of it is prime.
It doesn't matter what your age,
Just to the fullest life engage.
To your warmth and friendship we can attest.
We wish you only the best.

.

~60 Years Old -2

Wow, you are turning six oh!
So, we really want you to know,
That we wish you all the best,
And you really do deserve a day of rest.
Half way to a hundred and twenty you are,
So as much as it seems bizarre,
You have only lived half your life so far.
So forget the salad bar,
Open a good bottle of wine,
And go out and dine.
Now you can reap the reward,
Of all that you slaved over on the drawing board.
Sixty is a great age,
From everything that we can gauge.
The hard work is done,
It is time for some fun!
Enjoy the second half of your life,
We hope that with it there will be minimum strife.
We wish you all the best,
And hope that the rest of your life will be blessed.

~60 Years Old -3

So, this year you celebrate the big six oh
And upon your face we definitely see a special glow.
To celebrate you have decided to volunteer
Throughout the year.
This is just one more indication of how special you are,
And why in our books you are a real star.
You really deserve to feel fulfilled,
And to do many things that leave you thrilled.

~60 Years Old -4

Everyone wants to wish you *"Congratulations" today
Because you have lived your life in an exemplary way.
So don't worry about the number of candles on your cake.
Remember that life is all about what you do when you are awake.
You have helped so many people in your life
(And you have a great wife.)
Now we would like to do something to honor you
So a donation to **the Food Bank we attended to.
We wish you good health and lots of reasons to smile
And many moments that are worthwhile.
May you have a year low in stress
And high in spiritual success!!

*Can write "Mazel Tov".
**Write name of charity.

65 Years Old

So you are now sixty-five,
And very much alive!!
We hope that you will have a great day,
And that your whole year will go well in every way!

70 Years Old

~70 Years Old -1

Seventy years old you are now,
And all we can say is WOW!
But really only one year older you have become,
So perhaps you need not feel so numb.
Another year of experiences and joys you have had,
So for all the extra good times in your life you should be glad.
And now, if you don't want to do something just say, "Oy, I am so old",
Yet you are still young enough to have many adventures unfold.
Make the best out of the rest of your life.
Try to keep a low level to your strife.
May you be able to deal easily with any complication that arises,
And may you continually get good surprises.
May many things make you smile,
And not much make you hostile.
Enjoy your friends,
When the need arises make amends.
Wisely use your time,
Because all of it is prime.
May good adventures come your way,
And may you have at least a little fun every single day!
New experiences you should have plenty,
And blessings to count we hope you have many.
We hope that this year brings you many reasons to smile,
And that you do many special things that you find worthwhile.
It doesn't matter what your age,
Just to the fullest life engage.
We wish you all the best.
We hope that the rest of your life will be blessed.

~70 Years Old -2

I want to dedicate this to a special person who is turning seven oh.
There are some things that I really want you to know.
With you I really am impressed.
And I really do wish you the best.
You have not thought of life as a game.
You have always thought of what you wanted and taken aim.
You have really excelled.
High principles you have upheld.
You are really quite courageous.
To be your *daughter was rather advantageous.
Upon my life you have made a real impact.
Learning, travelling, always doing things in your life you have jam-packed.
Upon you maybe has snuck old age
But I know that you will tackle it with rage.
I hope that now you can reap the reward
Of all that you slaved over on the drawing board.
Seventy is a great age,
From everything that I can gauge.
The hard work is done.
It is time for some fun!
Enjoy the rest of your life.
May it be free of strife.
I wish you all the best.
I hope that the rest of your life will be blessed.

*You can change the relationship to friend, son, husband, wife, etc

74 Years Old

So you are turning seventy-four!
Well nobody can say that your life has been a bore.
You have seen so many places,
And put smiles on so many faces.
*We wish you another year of joy.
A special one with your first great grandchild who will be a special
little girl or boy.

*You can leave out the last two lines if they are not appropriate.
Remember that you can always take lines from other poems and add
them on.

75 Years Old

~75 Years Old -1

You're turning 75,
And you just seem to thrive!
Whatever you're doing seems tried and true,
So continue what you like to do.
Good health we wish for you
And that a lot more happy memories you will accrue.

~75 Years Old -2

You have a heart of gold,
And you really don't act 75 years old!

77 Years Old

Seven is the number of perfection,
And we all look up to you with affection.
It's hard to believe that you're turning seventy-seven this year,
You keep up a busy pace and your calendar is never clear.
Best wishes for a very special year we pass on to you,
Hoping that this year brings lots of good memories for you to
accrue.

80 Years Old

~80 Years Old -1

You have taught us to use our mind
So that in everything a good thing we can find.
So this year we get to take
A bigger piece of cake
Because we need more space
To hold enough candles to signify the years which you did
embrace.

For us you always open your arms wide.
Security, love and advice you do provide.
We love just sitting by your side.
To be your *grandchildren we feel pride.

It is hard to believe that you are now eighty years old.
You sure don't fit into a mold.
You really use your time well.
At this game of life you are swell.
That you continue to be healthy is our hope
And that with whatever comes your way you continue to cope.

*Can be changed to relative, friend, son, daughter, cousin,
children, etc.

~80 Years Old -2

So far you have lived 80 years long,
And we can see that you are still going strong!
Your body may not be quite as fast,
But a lot of wisdom you have amassed.
For your good health we pray
And that we love you we want to say.

90 Years Old

~90 Years Old -1

You are turning 90 years old
And you are still bold.
You say what you feel
And for help you still don't make an appeal.
Perhaps your body isn't what it once was,
But we can still hear your brain buzz.
Stay strong,
Keep moving along.
We are by your side
With pride.
Know that it is true
That we really do love you!

~90 Years Old -2

I have always been proud to be your *niece,
And as time goes on that pride does only increase.
In your lifetime you have really been influential.
You are one of those rare people who have lived up to their
potential.
Your special deeds have been somewhat noted,
And upon you some recognition has been promoted.
Although respect you did not pursue,
It has been bestowed upon you.
You have been like a **father to me,
And advice you did give every time I did plea.
A ninetieth birthday is so special to share,
Especially with someone like you, about whom we all do very
much care.

*If this is not for an aunt or uncle leave out the first two lines.
**Can be changed to mother, sister, brother or, "You have been a
friend to me".

98 Year's Old

It is amazing that you are turning ninety-eight
And you look so great!
You are so with it and it is easy to see,
That overall with life you are as happy as can be.

100 Years Old

As a child you must have laughed
That on the moon or mars could land any kind of spacecraft.
Yet here you are 100 years old
Having witnessed so many changes that did unfold.
Yet I can proclaim
That as far back as I can remember you looked the same.
You must have taken a potion
That keeps your brain in motion.
We are glad that we have this chance
To say that our lives you did enhance.
Many more healthy years we wish for you
And that more good memories you do accrue.
We hope that you know that it is true
That we really do love you!

Grandfather Who Would Have Turned 100

To my grandfather who was a special man,
Today we celebrate your life span.
To one hundred years,
We would like to offer our cheers.
*You were not very tall in height,
But many warm memories you did ignite.
*I can still see you skipping rope.
I knew that to skip faster or longer for me, there was no hope.
But you gave me hope in other ways,
And your love for us was always ablaze.
You taught me that school is not the only place for learning,
That the most important thing is the yearning.
Though you are no longer here
Your memory we still revere.

*If not appropriate this line and the following corresponding line
can be removed.

102 Years Old

To my dear *grandmother who is turning 102,
We really do look up to you.
You have really used your time well on earth,
And given your life a lot of worth.
You taught **scrabble to me,
And our time together I always looked forward to with glee.
We often met for tea,
And your stories always charmed me.
Friends you have never lacked,
Simply because you were never afraid to make contact.
I want to take this opportunity to say,
That even thinking of you adds to my day.
May you continue to be healthy and cognizant of everything that
goes on,
We really admire how you can go on so long without even a yawn.
You have shown that you do not take health for granted,
And to others this value you have also implanted.
I already can't wait until you turn 103,
For at that party I will also come and that is a guarantee.
And there is one other thing that I would like to say out loud,
And this is something of which I am very proud.
My life you really did touch,
And I love you very much.

*Feel free to change the relationship.
**Fill in something appropriate e.g. cooking, knitting, patience,
cards, etc.

Belated Wishes

~Belated -1

Okay *Bill, what can we say?
Your next birthday is already on the way!!!
But we really did and still do want to celebrate with you,
We so hope that over this delay you haven't been blue.

We are in awe of your early morning rising,
And we value your advising.
We all love coming in to your smiling face,
It is almost like a morning embrace.

We really value your attitude,
And hope for your kindnesses you feel our gratitude.
Of course we wish you good health for what's left of the year and
beyond,
And that at least one of your wishes comes true with the wave of a
wand.

We hope that this year brings you many reasons to smile,
And that you do many special things that you find worthwhile.
May you sleep well at night
Knowing that to us and many others you are a real delight!

*Write person's name.

~Belated -2

Your birthday is already past,
But that doesn't mean that for you our wishes have not amassed.
We wish for you a special year,
One of adventures and good times sitting around drinking beer.
Enjoy planning your life, your next meal and everything in-between.
The important thing is not to have everything a routine.
Remember adventure begins when work is done.
So take care to stay healthy but make sure to have fun!

~Belated -3

We want to wish you a very happy birthday,
And to celebrate with you even if there was a delay.
We hope that this will be a very special year for you
And that many adventures you will have time to pursue.
We truly wish you all the best,
In this coming year and generally in your life's quest!

~Belated -4

Though your birthday is finished,
Our wishes have not diminished.
*We wish for you a year of joy,
With lots of special moments with your little boy.
*Good luck with your new house,
We hope that you have many special times there with your spouse.
May this year bring you many things about which to smile,
And many activities which you feel are worthwhile.

*This rhyming couplet may be removed if it is not relevant.

~Belated -5

Even though your birthday was *two weeks ago,
We hope that you still feel that this **lunch in your honor is apropos.
After all it is only *two weeks late,
But we are hoping that with anticipation you did wait.
Truth be told we have been wishing you the best all along.
May you always feel in health and in soul to be strong!

*Write an amount of time or "a while".
**Can be changed to party, dinner, get-together, etc.

~Belated -6

Your birthday has come and gone,
But from our thoughts it has not been withdrawn.
May you spend time and resources on yourself,
Because if you don't you shouldn't expect it from any elf.
We hope that this year will bring with it many happy times,
And happy events which warrant rhymes.
Adventures we don't have to tell you to seek,
With this just continue with whatever is your technique.
We truly wish you all the best,
Keep living life with all your zest!

~Belated -7

*April seemed to sneak in,
And without me knowing it your birthday did begin.
I sure hope that it is not too late,
To wish you good things for your special date.
I wish you lots of happy times,
Even if for all of them you don't receive rhymes.
May you have lots of occasions which make you smile,
And lots of special experiences which are worthwhile.
May you be kept far from strife,
And may you feel satisfied with life.

*Write name of month.

~Belated -8

So *my dear friend your birthday has come and gone,
However, our wishes for you have not been withdrawn.
A lot of interesting trips we wish for you,
And that many new adventures you do accrue.
Health for you and your family is of course number one,
Without, it is hard to trek and have fun.
With a new grandchild on the way,
We hope that you will have much joy with the baby when **grandma
you do play.
We hope that this year will be full of just good things for you
And that lots of good memories you accrue!

*Put person's name or relationship (cousin, sister, etc.)
**Can be changed to grandpa, grandmother, grandfather, etc.
Remember that you can take out this and the corresponding line if
they are not appropriate.

Best Wishes From Far Away

~From Far Away -1

I value you and our friendship,
And enjoy our time when one of us visits on a trip.
I really enjoy conversing with you,
On the phone or by email when you are not in view.
I hope that for you this is a very special year,
Filled with lots of moments that you will always hold dear.
May you feel that you get lots of things done,
And be blessed with health, happiness and lots of fun

~From Far Away -2

We wish for you a very special day.
We are so sorry that from you we are far away,
But as you know people have to go their own way.

But just because we cannot be seen,
That we do not care is not what it does mean,
As to help you celebrate we truly are keen.

Good health we ask for you,
That many good wishes you do accrue,
And that your dreams you do pursue.

May you celebrate many more healthy years.
May you enjoy many good *wines with your peers,
And may you have many happy occasions to which your family
appears.

*You may substitute anything that the person likes: books, movies,
meals, classes, etc.

~From Far Away -3

Your birthday has once again come around,
And I felt that I should say something profound.
However, all I could think of were wishes to bestow upon you,
And that to say thank you for all of your help was overdue.
All of us over here,
Are wishing you a very meaningful year.
Of course we wish for you good health,
And that you realize that of good points you have a wealth.
New experiences you should have plenty,
And blessings to count, we hope you have many.
May this year be a fulfilling one.
May you feel fortunate even before it is done.
Go and just plain have fun.
Remember that a brand new year has begun.
We are sorry that we are not celebrating with you.
In your honor we will eat a piece of cake and that will have to do.

~From Far Away -4

Once again it's your birthday,
And we're far away.
But we all wish you a healthy year,
And good wishes that are sincere.
You and all the family in health should be well,
And have lots of good things to tell.
One year older you have become,
And perhaps this makes you a little numb.
But really another year of experiences and joys you have had.
So for all the extra good times in your life you should be glad.
Of course we wish for you many more,
With your children and your grandchildren who we know you adore.
May you be able to deal easily with any complication that arises,
And may you continually get good surprises.
We hope that you do not have to do too many things that you loath.
Rather this year should be one of spiritual growth.
Of course we all wish you the best,
And all of the other birthday wishes with zest!
May good adventures come your way,
And may you have at least a little fun every single day!

SMS Message/Twitter

~Message -1

Happy Birthday to you,
Many dreams this year may you pursue,
And much happiness may you accrue.

~Message -2

We want to wish you a happy birthday.
May good things come your way.
May you find much laughter
And may you live happily ever after!

~Message -3

No matter what you do tonight,
We hope that it will be to you a delight!

~Message -4

Cheers to you,
Many wishes we hope that you accrue.

~Message -5

We remember that it's your birthday today,
And we hope that you feel spoiled in at least some little way.

~Message -6

We all want to wish you a happy birthday,
Cause today is the day.
May you enjoy it and every day this year in a special way!

~Message -7

This is just a little birthday card,
To let you know that over your happiness we are standing on guard.

~Message -8

You always have a smile for anyone you meet.
-We can describe you in one word as sweet.

Rhyming Couplets Of 4 Lines

~4 Lines -1

This is just a little birthday token,
Hoping that our friendship is never broken.
May your year be full of nice surprises,
And may you be able to deal with anything that arises.

~4 Lines -2

We wish you a great year,
With lots of reason to cheer.
Be healthy, happy, and enjoy your gift.
We hope that it gives your life a little lift.

~4 Lines -3

We hope that your birthday is great,
And to it your whole family does relate.
Now that you are older and wiser,
To all of us you can be an advisor.

~4 Lines -4

Today is your birthday we're glad to say,
And we wish to celebrate with you in a small way,
Our birthday wishes will come at a later time,
But for now we hope that you will be happy with this little rhyme.

~4 Lines -5

With this I.O.U.
We hope that you will not be blue.
May this year be for you very fulfilling,
Doing lots of things that are thrilling!

~4 Lines -6

Happy Birthday to you,
We hope that a lot of good wishes you do accrue.
May you have a really good day,
And an excellent year that is terrific in every way.

~4 Lines -7

We wish you health and happiness on your birthday.
Celebrate with *Bill in a special way.
Be good to each other,
And enjoy being a mother!

*Write name of husband.

~4 Lines -8

There's more to a birthday than getting old.
It is also about on life getting a hold.
So over all that you have accomplished you should give a thought,
And we want to add that we all like you a lot.

~4 Lines -9

May you be blessed all year,
With an abundance of cheer!
May your problems be few,
But good times accrue!

~4 Lines -10

It's your birthday all day long,
And I hope that all year nothing goes wrong.
But if something happens to be even not quite right,
May you be able to carry on with inner strength and insight.

~4 Lines -11

It's your birthday all day long.
We sure hope that at least once you get sung a birthday song.
All day just smile, joke and have fun,
After all, today is celebrating that by no means is your life done.

~4 Lines -12

It's your birthday
So from your desk we want to take you away.
Please come for lunch with us
So over you we can make a little fuss.

~4 Lines -13
Working here we cannot promise you wealth,
But we can hope for you good health.
We are all wishing you a happy birthday
Hoping many good things come your way.

~4 Lines -14

At *ten o'clock we want you to take a little break
So that we can celebrate your birthday with some cake.
We are all wishing you a great year,
With lots of things that will bring you good cheer.

*Can change the time.

~4 (Okay this one is really 5) Lines -15

Today we are trying to put a smile on your face,
That throughout the year you will not erase.
But if you're down, just think of us,
And how over you we did make a fuss,
(And I sure hope that you don't cuss!)

Rhyming Couplets Of 6 Lines

~6 Lines -1

May you be blessed all year,
With an abundance of cheer!
May your problems be few,
And good times accrue!
May you have few trials,
But lots and lots of smiles!

~6 Lines -2

Happy Birthday – today is your day,
But then again, all year you seem to do things your way.
However we do want to proclaim
That we love you just the same.
But perhaps this year you could try,
To be not quite so much of a wise guy.

~6 Lines -3

We understand that today is your special day,
So good wishes we want to convey.
We hope that your whole year is sweet,
So as a token we have brought you a little treat.
We also want to thank you for all of the attention that you pay us,
We hope that besides our thanks our company is a plus!!!!!!!!

~6 Lines -4

You're whole family is together on your birthday,
So let's celebrate without delay!
Above all we wish you good health,
And we know that for you we better throw in a measure of wealth.
May you have an interesting fulfilling year,
Meeting lots of new people with whom you like going out to have a beer.

~6 Lines -5

Another year has passed,
And we know that a lot more recipes you have amassed.
We hope that this year you get to try some new exciting food,
And when you think about the recipes, us you do include.
But most of all we hope that you have a healthy fulfilling year,
One that has a lot of cheer!

~6 Lines -6

On a day which is sunny
We hope that you will use this money
To take your wife,
Which we hope is the love of your life,
Out for a meal
Which we hope will be ideal!

~6 Lines -7

So today is your birthday,
And in *two days you are going away.
It's hard to get a better gift,
As seeing **your grandchildren will be a real lift.
We wish you a special year,
Full of lots of cheer!

*You can change the amount of time.
**You can change this to seeing anybody specific or the name of a
place.

~6 Lines -8

We wish for you to be healthy and strong,
Especially because we know that your days are very long.
May this year continue to bring you many happy times,
With lots of occasions to receive rhymes.
Continue to be relaxed with life,
Keeping far from you any strife.

~6 Lines -9

We hope that you are pleased with your birthday food dishes,
And more importantly that come true at least some of your birthday
wishes.
We hope that health wise you will be well,
And that you live life to its fullest and not under a spell.
Finally we hope that no matter what comes your way,
You will remember that we are here for you every day.

~6 Lines -10

Happy birthday to you!
Soon in your arms you will hold someone new.
We wish for you an easy birth,
But no matter what we are sure you will feel the worth.
May you be well,
And everything just swell!

~6 Lines -11

We all hope that on your birthday you have a great day,
Getting a lot of attention and that the whole day is lively and gay.
We wish for you good health and lots of fun times,
And many special occasions deserving rhymes.
So – no procrastination –
Go and start your celebration!

~6 Lines -12

We hope for you and your family health for this year and beyond,
And that as a family you continue to bond.
Personally, may you feel satisfied with life,
And receive joy from your kids and your wife.
May good adventures come your way,
And may you have at least a little fun every single day!

~6 Lines -13

This is just a short birthday note,
So that you don't feel that strangled feeling in your throat
Thinking that we forgot and would let today slip away,
Without wishing you happy birthday in any way.
We hope that at least today you have been treated well,
Though we hope that your whole year will be swell.

~6 Lines -14

We hope that you leave work early today
To celebrate your birthday in some special way.
Go out for dinner,
Or just open a bottle of wine that is a winner.
It doesn't matter much as long as some celebration you create
Because for your birthday we want you in a joyous state.

~6 Lines -15

At *2:30 we will all shirk
Our work
To wish you a happy birthday
In the proper way.
So 'till then don't be blue,
We are all thinking of you!

*Fill in the correct time.

Rhyming Couplets Of 8 Lines

~8 Lines -1

You are really a good friend,
And you help me with everything that I have to contend.
I always feel that to me you have an open door,
Because of you I can do ever so much more.
You are always there in the time of my need,
Without you I really could not succeed.
On your birthday I wish for you a special day
With a whole year of good things on the way!

~8 Lines -2

This is a special birthday and we are so glad that we are near,
Because in our hearts you are truly dear.
We wish good health for you,
And some adventures to pursue.
May you be surrounded by friends,
And enjoy good times by the tens.
May this be for you a great year,
Full of nothing but good cheer!

~8 Lines -3

It's your birthday today,
So we're going to tell you what we have to say.
That you're here again is a gift to us,
And we're glad you're not going away for a while in a plane or on a
bus.
So today enjoy some cake,
And know that our wishes to you really are not fake.
We hope for you special things happen this year,
And you know that if you ever need anything we will be near.

~8 Lines -4

So, this weekend you have another celebration
To add to this year's elation.
Make sure that you take time for yourself once in a while,
So that you can keep your smile.
Keep an eye on all the good in your life,
To help keep away any feeling of strife.
We wish for you health and good cheer,
With lots of good things all year!

~8 Lines -5

So it's your birthday
And we just want to say:
We hope that you have a great year,
With lots of reasons to cheer.
In health may you be well,
And in general may your year be swell!
May it be a year low in stress,
And high in success!

~8 Lines -6

You are so terrific it is hard to believe,
So at least on your birthday accolades you should receive.
We love you a lot,
And although it may seem it your birthday was not forgot.
We're sorry that your gift is not on hand,
And we hope that you will be happy right now with our vocal band.
So we'll sing to you day and night,
Until we buy your gift and make it right.

~8 Lines -7

Happy birthday to you,
A lot of things for you this year will be new.
You will be going to a new school,
And we hope that to you the kids will be cool.
We value that you are a person that can be relied upon,
And wish you the strength for many adventures to embark on.
If you need us we will be there for a crutch.
We hope that you know that we all love you very much.

~8 Lines -8

To our dear *friend who everyone does revere,
We hope that you have many special moments this year.
Good health we are wishing for your family and you,
Although about your gift we are not going to give you any clue.
That you will enjoy your gift we have little doubt.
What it is we can't wait for you to find out.
In general enjoy your life as it is probably the only one that you will
receive,
And good luck with what you want to achieve.

*You can fill in the person's name or relation.

~8 Lines -9

To a new apartment you are about to move,
And with this new location we hope your life does improve.
It certainly seems that your year is starting in a special way,
And we hope that your birthday will be a great day.
We hope that you have a healthy year,
And that every once in a while good surprises appear.
We can't wait to see you
And celebrate your birthday anew!

~8 Lines -10

It seems to us that you had a birthday last year too,
But that's okay as we like to celebrate with you.
May your garden bloom,
But too much of your time we hope that it does not consume.
May your garden always look its best,
And may it help you feel at rest.
We hope that for your birthday you get served some tasty dishes
And of course we wish you all of the traditional birthday wishes.

~8 Lines -11

Tomorrow is your big day,
And we hope that you do something special even if it is just to go to
a café.
This year you have decided to shake up the status quo,
And in your life some changes you will undergo.
We hope that this year will be just great,
And that you will keep us up-to-date.
Your health should be the best,
And in anything you decide to do you should be blessed!

~8 Lines -12

So it's your birthday once again this year,
And we want you to know that our good wishes are very sincere.
We hope that you get to travel with *Jill to many interesting places,
And see many events which light up your faces.
Of course good health we wish for you both,
As well as spiritual growth.
That your goals you do achieve,
And that you always have something in which to believe.

*Fill in name of spouse, partner, your children, etc.

~8 Lines -13

It's your birthday today,
And we hope that you spend it in a special way.
Of course we hope that *Bill has something nice planned for you.
If not this is an issue that we will need to pursue.
We did miss talking in the morning with you,
But at least we hope that on a good breakfast you did chew.
Make sure that for yourself you do something,
And enjoy all the nice surprises that this day does bring.

*Fill in name of partner, or write your children, your family, etc.

~8 Lines -14

I hope that for you this will be a special day,
You really deserve much health and happiness without delay.
Of others you are always thoughtful and considerate and kind,
So I hope that on this day extra happiness you do find.
May your dreams come true for the good,
And may you feel understood.
May every day bring to you a special delight,
And may you know that you help make my life bright.

~8 Lines -15

Today is your birthday,
And there are some special things that we would like to say.
Like we wish you good health,
And to do the important things you have enough wealth.
We hope that you have a special day,
And that good things come your way.
Over you it is worth making a fuss.
Happy birthday from all of us!

~8 Lines -16

You have proven year after year,
That to high moral standards you adhere.
You always keep busy,
You almost make us dizzy.
May something special come your way,
Every single day.
May you never go astray.
May you know that for your health and happiness we do pray.

~8 Lines -17

It is your birthday.
But we are happy to say that you are not showing any decay.
For your birthday may your house be clean,
And your family treat you like a queen.
May all the hopes and wishes your family have for you,
Come true.
May your special day feel like a dance,
With everything going just right as you move in a trance
.

~8 Lines -18

We hope that for you this is a successful year;
One that is good for yourself, your family and your career.
May you feel that you are still *biking hard and strong,
And that with the leaders you still belong.
But should it happen that your age starts slowing you down,
Feel certain that upon you we will not frown.
We hope that this year brings very few defeats,
And that it is filled with good health and many treats.

*You could change this to something else that fits in appropriately
(playing tennis, playing golf, etc.

~8 Lines -19

May this year see at least one of your wishes fulfilled,
And may many things leave you feeling thrilled.
In your life,
May you not have much strife.
For you a feeling of harmony and fulfillment we wish,
And that something tasty is on every dinner dish.
For you and your family may this be a healthy year,
And we want you to know that if you need us we are always near.

~8 Lines -20

I hope that for you this will be a special day.
You really do deserve much health and happiness without delay.
Of others you are always thoughtful and considerate and kind,
So I hope that on this day extra happiness you do find.
May your dreams come true for the good.
May you feel that you are understood.
I would like to thank you for making my days so bright,
And I hope that every day brings to you a special delight!

~8 Lines -21

Today is your day, so with you everyone should agree,
But not everything in this world is as it should be.
However, your work and your gentle way,
Has never led us astray.
With a polite manner you help things get done,
Yet you also remember that it is important to have fun.
We all wish you a healthy year,
With lots of good wishes which are sincere.

Rhyming Couplets Of More Than 8 Lines

~More Than 8 Lines -1

Some people would say,
That today is just like any other day.
But we know that birthdays
Are special in so many ways.
They are days on which we can reflect,
And think of those who have helped us with respect.
Yet we also look ahead,
With a special kind of hope that holds no dread.
Our birthdays may be known,
But there is something about them that is a private stepping stone.
May this year see you fulfill some of your dreams,
And set up new schemes.
Of course a birthday is also a time that good wishes others express,
So we wish you a healthy year, filled with good cheer, without any
stress.

~More Than 8 Lines -2

I think that a birthday is a good time to check and see
What we have accomplished and to what degree.
A birthday is a celebration of your life
Of the good deeds and accomplishments which are rife.
So don't worry about the number of candles on your cake.
Remember that life is all about what you do when you are awake!
You are always moving ahead,
So a birthday to you should not be dread,
But rather celebrated without fear
As you used your time well year after year.
See what new adventures will appear
And stay young for yet another year!
Wisely use your time,
Because all of it is prime.
It doesn't matter what your age,
Just to the fullest life engage.
We hope that this year brings you many reasons to smile,
And that you do many special things that you find worthwhile.
Of course we all wish you the best,
And all of the other birthday wishes with zest!
Go and just plain have fun!
Remember that a brand new year has begun.

~More Than 8 Lines -3

May you have much joy from your kids and your husband too.
Many good memories this year may you accrue.
With your life may you feel content,
And may you have someone willing to listen when you need to vent.
May you feel great meaning in your life,
And may you be kept away from strife.
May you have good health all year long.
May you feel physically and spiritually strong.
May this year be filled with many things that get you to smile,
And many moments that you deem worthwhile.
May you have a great year,
And may your worries disappear.
May it be a year low in stress,
And high in success!

~More Than 8 Lines -4

We're glad that today you are not away,
As we want to send you some wishes without delay!
We wish for you lots of days when your house stays clean,
And each of your children treats you as a queen.
May you find that as your children grow,
Upon you more and more respect they bestow.
May you enjoy many new dances,
And feel that in life you are making advances.
Just as you asked we are not making a big fuss,
But we are wishing you a happy birthday from all of us.

~More Than 8 Lines -5

So it is your birthday again.
We think that you had another though we can't remember when.
Perhaps it was about this time last year.
Well, we'll celebrate again so don't you fear.
You are certainly an important part of our team.
We hold you in very high esteem.
We love your way of finding out details,
And telling us all of the tales.
In person, or on the phone,
You find a connection that no one else would have known.
As you have a special way,
To get someone their family history to convey.
We listen carefully waiting for the twist and turn.
For these we really do yearn.
After each phone conversation you seem to have something to recall,
And with each story us you do enthrall.
But aside from your work and your stories, we want you to know,
That as a person our praise of you does overflow.
Important you make everybody feel.
The good in everyone you seem to reveal.
To others comfort you always bring,
So we hope that this year in your step there will be an extra spring.
To your fullest live your life,
Enjoy your children, grandchildren and being *Bill's wife.

*Fill in name of husband or write "and your wife" for a man.

~More Than 8 Lines -6

Today is your birthday,
And we hope that lots of good things are on your way!
Children who listen,
A house that does glisten.
Lots of happy times,
That don't cost too many dimes.
Good health,
And an understanding that the most important thing is not wealth.
May you always have someone in which to confide,
And good friends by your side.

~More Than 8 Lines -7

Happy birthday on this special day.
We know that you rather play,
But you are with us at work,
Your responsibilities you did not shirk.
We hope that you feel at peace
And that your joy in life does nothing but increase.
We hope you feel fulfillment in your life,
And that you don't have much strife.
We all wish you a healthy year,
And good wishes which are sincere.

~More Than 8 Lines -8

We wanted to buy something that would make you happy.
We certainly didn't want to get you something crappy.
So we thought perhaps we would get you something that would be
cozy and warm,
Even if outside there was a storm.
So we racked our brains.
In fact it felt like we were having labor pains.
And then the idea did come,
That a *cozy towel may help you cheerfully hum.
May you have a good year,
With lots of cheer!

*You can substitute something for the cozy towel

~More Than 8 Lines -9

We would like to celebrate with you your birthday,
And so we thought that from your *desk we could pull you away.
One year older you have become,
And perhaps this makes you a little numb.
But really another year of experiences and joys you have had,
So for all the extra good times in your life you should be glad.
Of course we wish for you many more,
With your husband, your children and your grandchildren who we
know you adore.
May you be able to deal easily with any complication that arises,
And may you continually get good surprises.
We hope that you do not have to do too many things that you loath
And that this year is one of spiritual growth!

*You can substitute house, books, computer, tennis, etc.

~More Than 8 Lines -10

You are generous in so many ways,
And your love of life is always ablaze!
You are satisfied with the little things in life,
Like looking at the stars, drinking wine and being to *Bill a wife.
Your smile is always aglow,
And in the morning we have to smile too when you say, "Hello."
Yet from serious subjects you do not shy away.
You are well informed and your opinions you know how to convey.
You add warmth to any room that you are in,
And certainly being your friend is for us a win.

*Fill in the husband's name, or for a man instead of "being to Bill a wife" write, "with your wife."

~More Than 8 Lines -11

Sometimes you're life is so busy,
That it kind of makes us dizzy.
So we thought of a gift,
That will help your gears shift.
We hope that after all of your running around,
It helps you wind down.
Don't forget to smile,
And take time to do what is really worthwhile.
May you feel that every day,
Something good has come your way!

~More Than 8 Lines -12

To you there is always a lot to say,
You are so giving and considerate and you wear a smile every day!
With people you really know how to talk,
And among nature you love to walk.
Your stories we love to hear,
Whether they are about your family, a stranger or how you went out
to drink beer.
There is no doubt that you know in importance health is number
one,
And that without a *vitamin, a day has not really begun.
So since you have your priorities set,
We would like you to know that your birthday we could never forget!
Our good wishes we want to pass on to you:
May good health and blessings meet you each day anew.
May you enjoy with your family many happy times,
And may there be many good reasons to write you rhymes!

* Fill in something appropriate like coffee, sandwich, kiss and hug,
newspaper, etc.

~More Than 8 Lines -13

You can always make us smile,
Because in any situation you can find something worthwhile.
Why something happened you understood,
And lunch is always really good.
Thank you for your positive vibrations,
They help us in life with our evaluations.
We hope for you that your wishes come out for the best,
And that this year you progress in your life's quest.
May you feel in body and mind to be whole,
And that over your life you are at least mainly in control.

.~More Than 8 Lines -14

You have a great smile,
Which takes you that extra mile.
You often give us food for thought,
And we love you a lot.
You are definitely unique
And demand attention when you speak.
You are full of lots of life
And when the time is right you will make a great wife.
May this year be for you great.
May you be able to handle everything that you want to put on your plate.
May you be well and whole,
In body and soul!

~More Than 8 Lines -15

Your big day has arrived,
And of our birthday wishes we do not want you to be deprived.
This is sure to be a busy year,
With new grandchildren far and near.
We are sure that it will be a year full of smiles and lots of fun,
And hope that you will feel that you have gotten things done.
We wish good health for you,
And some adventures to pursue.
May you be surrounded by family and friends,
And enjoy good times by the tens.
May this be simply for you a great year,
Full of nothing but good cheer!

~More Than 8 Lines -16

This lunch is dedicated to you,
And one more birthday that you did now accrue.
But by no means think that anyone would mistake you for getting
old,
Because we all know that you still have much energy to unfold.
Of course we know that you like to spoil everyone,
Because, simply for you, it is fun.
So today we would like to spoil you just a bit,
And a few appreciative words to you we would like to transmit.
So thank you for *all the calories that we have gained due to the
pastries that you have made for us,
And informing us of all the great places around the country which
you find and feel are a plus.
**We like that you share with us your special roses,
And thank you for letting us smell them close to our noses.
But most of all we want you to know,
That we wish for you a year full of health and happiness and that
your fulfillment does grow.

*You can change this to anything appropriate e.g. for all the help that
you gave us.
**If not appropriate you can remove this line and the next.

~More Than 8 Lines -17

Don't worry about the number of candles on your cake,
Or even any minor ache.
Remember that life is all about what you do when you are awake!

May you have good health all year long.
May you feel physically and spiritually strong,
And may life go along like a song.

May you always have good friends to share your joy,
And many experiences to enjoy.

May this year be filled with many things that get you to smile,
And many moments that you deem worthwhile.

May you have a great year,
And your worries disappear.

May it be a year low in stress,
And high in success!

May this be simply for you a great year,
Full of nothing but good cheer!

~More Than 8 Lines -18

Time seems to have slipped away
And once again it is your birthday.
Live it up big time
While you're in your prime!
Play hard and work hard,
But make sure that your family you do not disregard.
Hope that events this year keep you smiling
And that good times you keep compiling.
May you be healthy and happy,
And may life not be crappy!!

~More Than 8 Lines -19

May this year bring to you simplicity in finding parking spots,
And lunches that will not leave you distraught.
We hope that the kids wake up every morning without a fuss,
And that the dog is taken out for a walk without this you having to
discuss.
May life get a bit simpler for you, in short,
And may you feel that we give you at least a little support.
We wish you a great year,
With lots of reason to cheer.
Be healthy, happy, and enjoy your gift,
We hope that it gives your life a little lift.

~More Than 8 Lines -20

We can see that you are truly trying,
To keep from crying.
For on the table you do not see a present,
And this is causing you torment.
We really don't want to make you sad.
Then we would feel very bad.
So here is the deal,
We really do want to give you something with appeal.
But also different we wanted it to be,
And we hope that in the end you will agree.
We hope that our gift will make you smile,
Because for this special birthday we wanted to go the extra mile.

~More Than 8 Lines -21

We want to celebrate your birthday
In a special way
So we would like to invite you to lunch
Where we can talk and munch.
I'm sure that you know that the table will be set in a lovely display,
And the food will be as good as any café!
Are you willing to share with *Sue your special day?
As her birthday from yours is not far away,
For **Monday, April 21st this invitation is set.
So don't forget!
We can't wait to celebrate with you both in a special way,
Although we also hope that you will make a birthday wish today!!!

*Fill in other worker's name.
**Fill in proper day and date.

~More Than 8 Lines -22

I'm not sure why we celebrate the day that we are born,
Perhaps it is to warn us that wasted time we are to mourn.
We are to use our time well
And it is a push to get us to excel.
But you always have something on your plate
For a birthday you don't even need to wait.
You are always moving ahead
So a birthday to you should not be dread
But rather celebrated without fear
As you used your time well year after year.
*You've been just about everywhere around the globe
And the food and the wine you did probe.
You are not one to just lie around
You have people to see and things to do around town.
There are **more movies and restaurants you want to review I'm
sure,
I think that for aging you have found the cure!

*Leave this and the corresponding line out if not appropriate.
**Can substitute other things that the person likes to do for example
"many more museums that you would like to see I'm sure" or " many
more golf courses you would like to visit I'm sure," etc.

~More Than 8 Lines -23

To *Bill who just turned **57 years old
We think that you know that life is about more than just gold,
That there are many wonders to behold.

We hope that when your life you do review,
You find a lot of good memories you did accrue,
And that in your spirituality you grew.

We want you to know that you have friends by your side,
And we hope that you feel in us you can confide,
Especially when you have important things to decide.

We wish you a healthy year,
Filled with all sorts of good cheer,
And much success in your career.

*Change to appropriate name.
**Can change to any number.

~More Than 8 Lines -24

Today
Is your birthday
And we all want to shout,
"Run! Get out!"
But we know that you wouldn't leave
So, what would it achieve?
To your desk you would cleave
As in hard work you believe.
Stop choking!
Just joking!
We will try to make sure that you have a great day
So that tonight you will be in the mood to go out and play!

CHILD MOVING AWAY

To our *Jill who has grown so tall,
And can now almost control yourself in the mall.
Fashion you certainly do know.
This shows more and more as you grow.
Having you around is usually a pleasure,
And generally we do think of you as a treasure.
Seriously, we love you very much,
Even if you we are not allowed to touch.
Forming your own ideas you are,
And sometimes we think that they are quite bazaar.
Always agree we certainly will not,
But that does not keep us from loving you a lot.
Count on you all your friends know that they can,
Or come to you for a plan.
Thought of highly you really are,
And knowing your strong points we don't think that is at all bizarre.
Good luck in everything that you try to do.
I hope that you know we are always behind you.
We love you very much indeed,
And we know that when you try you have a good chance to succeed.
That you are our child we are very glad.
Love you a lot, from Mom and Dad.

*Change to name of child.

CLEANING THE HOUSE
(To be taped to a toy, book or game)

I guess that you don't like me anymore,
And I was so happy when you picked me in the store.
You keep leaving me everywhere,
And I am now in despair.

COMING BACK TO WORK AFTER AN ABSENCE

~Coming Back -1

It is great to have you back.
Without you we did feel a lack.
We missed you,
Talking and hearing your point of view.
You were definitely not forgot
And it is great having you back in your spot!

~Coming Back -2

To you we want to give a great big "hello",
Especially because the amount of work in this office is about to
grow.
We hope that you missed us at least a bit,
And simply that we're glad you're back we want to transmit.

CONTESTS

~Contest -1

Off to a competition you are to go,
And we know that you will not be slow.
So *run as fast as you can,
Knowing that we will be cheering for you as our man.

*Write the appropriate word- bike, row, pedal, etc.

~Contest -2

May you feel accomplished no matter what your feat.
We certainly hope that your victory will be complete,
And that all the others you do beat!

But if you do not come in number one,
We hope that at least you can look back and say that you did have
fun!

~Contest -3

Of course we wish you lots of luck.
We certainly hope that you do not get stuck,
Nor for any reason do you have to be put on a truck.

~Contest -4

Good luck on your ride.
May strength and luck be on your side.
We will all be thinking of you,
Hoping that lots of points you do accrue.
But if you don't come out on top,
It's okay, but keep pumping until you drop.

After a Contest

We sure hope that you had some fun,
Even if you were not the one that won.
We hope that you feel satisfied with your standing,
And that at no time did you have a crash landing.
We hope to hear a story or two,
About the race, the people and what you did view.

CORPORATE SPONSOR

As a corporate sponsor we consider you a truly special friend,
So to you an extra thank you we would like to extend.
Thanks to corporations like yours this world is a better place,
And we can see on more *children a smile on their face.

*Can change this to anything appropriate.

CUSTOMER RESPONSE

~Customer Response -1

To us you did not come back,
And we would really like to know what we did lack.
Value your comments we do,
Your advice we would like to pursue.
Please let us know why you did not return,
From your comments we would really like to learn.

~Customer Response -2

We would really like to know
If with you our service did rank high or low.
It is important to know what you feel
So that we can steadily improve until we are ideal!
Thanks for your time in filling out this questionnaire.
You can be sure that we will read it with care!

~Customer Response -3

We would like to know what we did wrong and what we did right
Because for your loyalty we are willing to fight!
Please fill out the form below
So how to improve we will know!

EMPLOYEE OF THE YEAR

What does it mean to be the employee of the year?
It means that someone's work we especially revere.
He or she has worked especially hard.
Often to personal time giving no regard.
Helping others with a smile.
Making you feel that every question and statement is worthwhile.
Work is done with special care,
And it is done with flair!
When I call this year's appointee,
Will he or she please stand up and stand beside me.

Voting for Employee of the Year

Please vote on who you think should be the employee of the year.
Someone who to their work has been very sincere.
It should be someone that you think has given their all
And upon whom for help you thought you could freely call.
Please hand in your vote in the coming days
For who you think deserves our praise.

ENGAGEMENT

~Engagement -1

Forward in life the two of you should walk side by side.
In each other you should feel free to confide.
Advice one to the other you should gently provide.
To reach new heights the other you can guide.
In each other may you always feel pride.
Little differences may you be able to set aside.
Major decisions together may you decide.

May a long and happy life unfold for you two.
Together, many endeavors may you pursue.
With many impromptu outbursts of one saying to the other, "I love
you".

~Engagement -2

Engaged you are now,
So your love you did avow.
We are very happy for both of you,
And hope that many good memories you do accrue.
May you always feel that each day is the best,
And may your union be blessed.

~Engagement -3

A daughter you have one,
And her days of living at home are about to be done.
For things have now been set,
And in *January a husband she will get.
So, congratulations from us all,
For **Jill the time has come to book a wedding hall.
Enjoy the planning,
It really can be enchanting.
Delight in **Jill's smiles.
May you not have too many trials.
Revel in the twinkle in ***Bill's eyes,
As he looks at **Jill and his love he cannot disguise.
Enjoy many years of pride from them.
May their life together be a real gem!

*You can change to the appropriate month of the wedding.
**Write in name of bride-to-be.
***Write in the name of the groom-to-be.

Engagement Announcement from the Parents

Congratulations to *Bill and me,
For *Jack and Jill we are as happy as can be!
We must have aged
Because we now have **a child engaged!

*Change to appropriate names.
**Can change to a different number of children.

From a Parent of the Bride-to-be to the New Couple

*Jill you were once our little girl,
Now before you a dream is beginning to unfurl.
** On your trip you have met the boy,
Who will bring you everlasting joy.
***Turkeys he will clean,
And hopefully make you feel like a queen.
On your engagement we do say,
Now ****Bill you are part of our family without delay.
I hope that together you will make many a dream.
Fulfill them and hold each other in high esteem.
May you always lend each other a hand,
And may you always listen to the other and try and understand.
For living together at times is hard,
But don't let your marriage be marred.
It will often need work,
And this you must not shirk.
Realize that marriage is a serious matter,
And know that for the two of you we couldn't be gladder.
May your love grow.
May you always be caught in Cupid's bow.
Soon you will both stand side-by-side,
And your lives will be modified.
Together you will be one,
And Daddy and I will finally have *****a son.
Now to being together which is your dream,
We all say *l'chaim*.

*Fill in the name of the bride-to-be
**Fill in the place that the couple met (At university, In Chicago, etc.)
***You can change turkey to something else or leave out this couplet
if it is not relevant.
****Fill in the name of the groom-to-be
*****Can change "a" to "another".

To the Parents of an Engaged Couple

We are so happy to know,
That your family is about to grow.
We wish *Jill, *Bill, the whole family and especially both of you,
Much pride and that much happiness together you do accrue.
Wishing you all the best,
And that this marriage will be blessed.

*Fill in the name of the engaged couple.

FEELING BLUE

~Feeling Blue -1

This is just something light,
To help make your eyes bright.
Whenever you are down,
Just think of a clown.
He wants to hand you a balloon,
But he is swept up to the moon.
Just as you are about to cry,
In his face he gets a pie.
He falls down to the ground,
And a lucky penny he has found.
He gives it to you,
And now you just can't be blue.

~Feeling Blue -2

Let all your worries be swept away.
Don't be upset all day.
Our good company we hope that you will enjoy,
And that away from your troubles we can be a decoy.

~Feeling Blue -3

We're sorry to hear that you hit a snag,
And that life has been such a drag.
But we hope that from now you can start anew,
And that you won't be so blue.
We are glad that in us you could confide.
We hope that some comfort we did provide.
We hope that life will easier get,
But no matter what happens remember that there is a reason that we
met.
Your friendship we value, we really do,
And no matter what, we are here to help you pull through.
So please don't hesitate to talk to us,
Whether we're at home, in the office, in the car, or in the bus.
No matter where you are we wish you the best,
And we'll always be around at the slightest request.

GET WELL

~Get Well -1

We are SOOOOOOOO glad that your tests came back clear.
Now all of your fears can disappear.
Our wish is for you to be healthy in every way,
And to be grateful for this every day.

~Get Well -2

That you are feeling better we are all glad,
Especially because we know that when you don't feel 100% you feel
a bit mad.
But your body takes time to heal,
And sometimes rest is ideal.
We're glad that you're energy level is coming back.
And that you are clearly back on track.

~Get Well -3

We feel so bad that you ache in your muscle.
We know that you really want to hustle.
And we're sure that this makes you feel down,
And we really hate to think of you with a frown.
Please accept this little token,
With our words that are sometimes unspoken.
We are thinking of you,
And wondering what we can do.
We want so much for you to smile.
Just realize that you are only in bed for awhile.
For now we know that you have to rest
So that soon you can get up and do your best.

~Get Well -4

We would like to let you know of our concern,
And our wish that with full strength to work you will return.

~Get Well -5

Welcome to the meeting,
You deserve a special greeting!
We know that you have been rather sick
And yet to come today you gave yourself a little kick.
We think that it is great that you are always so upbeat,
We wish you a recovery that is truly complete!

GIVING A PIN

Here is a pin that we hope you will wear with pride,
As you scatter worldwide.
We know that you have worked very hard,
And for all of your work we hold you in high regard.

GOING AWAY TO SCHOOL

We love you so much,
And we will really miss your kiss with the light touch.
But this is really an opportunity for you,
Which we are sure that you are equal to.
We're sure that the experience is a little bit scary,
But in a short time you will make new friends and be merry.
About us, please do not forget,
Or over your choice of schools we will really sweat.
Remember your values and do not sin.
Do not start smoking, or doping or drinking gin.
To yourself be true.
Don't do anything that you don't think you should do.
Be proud of who you are,
Know that in our eyes you are really a star.
By going to this school, much courage you are showing,
And we hope that from all you learn and experience you will be
glowing.
*You are certainly no longer a little girl,
We really give you a lot of credit for giving this school a whirl.
We will be thinking of you a lot,
But we will be content knowing that you are being given a lot of food
for thought.
Remember that to us you can always phone,
Whether day or night, or even if you are in the Twilight Zone.
You make us proud,
And we're glad to say that we love you aloud.

*For a boy take out this line and the next.

HOLIDAYS

Christmas

~Christmas -1

Christmas is a time to think of others,
Friends, sisters, brothers, fathers and mothers.
It is a time to give a token
For the words we have too seldom spoken,
"Thank you for all that you have done for me,
I appreciate you, even if we don't always agree."

~Christmas -2

I hope that Santa leaves you something good
Although I'm not quite sure that he should.
I understand that he often leaves coal,
To people who have not kept their lives under control.
And he knows if you have been good or bad
So if you get anything you should be glad!

~Christmas -3

May your Christmas be merry
And your life not be too scary.
May your new year be happy,
And nothing happen that is too crappy.
May Iran keep all of its toys within its borders
And suicide bombers learn not to follow orders.
May we know no war
And our biggest problem be cleaning the kitchen floor.

Father's Day

~Father's Day -1

On this Father's Day
I pray
That you know
That as I grow
Your advice means a lot to me
Even if we do not always agree.
Thank you for being my guide,
Always by my side,
But also letting me go my own way,
Living my own life every day.

~Father's Day -2

Thanks Dad,
For all that to my life you add.
For the big things and the small.
I know that on you I can always call.
You deserve my praise
For helping me in so many ways.
So sit back and enjoy today
Because tomorrow I expect you to help me in at least some little way.

~Father's Day -3

Today is Father's Day
So put your wallet away.
We're going out as our treat
And you can order anything that you would like to eat.
And for you we have this little gift
To give your life a lift.
Thanks for all that you do
And for just being you!

~Father's Day -4

Father's Day was set aside
So that on at least one day we would stand in pride
And say that I am glad
That you are my dad.
You do so much for me
In my life you are key.
Over helping me you never think twice
And you are always ready with advice.
I know that I do not say it enough,
But it is no bluff,
I love you!
Thank you for all that you do!!

~Father's Day -5

To my dad
Who makes me glad,
I'm sorry for when I'm bad,
Or I make you mad.

You mean a lot to me
And I know that if I need, you will make yourself free
Even if you know that I do not always agree.
In my life you are definitely key!

Thanks for all that you did do
Throughout the years as I grew.
I know that I am overdue
In saying, "Thank you."

Hannukah

~Hannukah -1

Hannukah is a celebration of lights,
A time when we strive for new heights.
We remember the Maccabees who were only a few
Yet they fought and many they did subdue.
Hannukah is a time to publicize that we can be strong
And fight against what we believe to be wrong.

~Hannukah -2

Many years ago the Maccabees felt that they had to attack,
And their freedom and their Temple they won back.
The Temple they did clean,
And once again the light from the oil was seen.
We thank them today
For helping keep the Jewish traditions from fading away.
Remember as your menorah you light
That it is up to you now to keep the Jewish traditions bright.

~Hannukah -3

On Hannukah food we do not boil,
We fry it in oil.
Nor do we sit in the dark at night,
We light candles for all to see burn bright.
For eight full days we celebrate with joy
Because the Syrian-Greeks the Maccabees did destroy.
They won back our Temple and our way of life,
So that we could live as Jews without the same strife.

~Hannukah -4

On Hannukah we gain a lot of weight
As we pile donuts and latkes on our plate.
And we burn lights for eight nights
To commemorate that the Maccabees fought for our rights.
With our dreidels we get to play,
To remember how the children used to watch for the enemy coming
their way.
We do all this to remember that for us the Maccabees fought
So that we could continue to carry on the laws and traditions that our
ancestors taught.

Mother's Day

~Mother's Day -1

To my mother on Mother's Day,
Thank you for helping me not go astray.
I hope for you that all your dreams come true for the best,
And that to many more good memories you can attest.
May my family and I bring you much joy,
And together many times may we enjoy.
Thanks for your help that you have given over the years to me,
That we will have many good things to celebrate together I hope you
can foresee.
Now, while we are all healthy,
And relatively wealthy,
Let's lift up our glasses for a toast,
To the mother that I love the most.

~Mother's Day -2

Happy Mother's Day,
And I want to say
Thank you in every way!

You were my mother from day number one,
And I'm sure that your worrying days are still not done,
But I hope that out of this relationship you get some pride and fun!

~Mother's Day -3

So once again the day has come
For us all to salute our mom.
An oxymoron Mother's Day seems
As moms slip into all of our dreams.
Just one day a year?
For someone so dear?
It must just be
That Mother's Day is a guarantee
That we stop for just a bit
And say thank you for all that moms transmit.
For all the help and advice
Without thinking twice.
For all the homemade and restaurant food
And for always trying to put us in a good mood.
Thank you
For all that you do.
That I appreciate you I want to convey
When, "Have a great Mother's Day" I say.

~Mother's Day -4

Years of caring are hard to repay,
The least I can do is say thank you today.
Thanks for all the food you prepared over the years,
And for all the times you abated my fears.
You gave all different kinds of aid,
And I'm sure at times you felt like a maid.
Know that I do appreciate all that you did do,
And I really do want to thank you!

~Mother's Day -5

Only once a year is there a Mother's Day
But there are not many days that I don't think of you in some way.

New Year

~New Year -1

We hope that this year,
Brings you much cheer,
That you have nothing to fear,
And that something that has puzzled you becomes clear.
May lots of good things come your way,
And may you have something to be thankful for every day.
May you have lots of occasions to smile,
And may you have the strength to walk that extra mile.
May you be well in body and mind,
And may life in general to you be kind.

~New Year -2

Let's hope that this new year,
Brings to all the world lots of cheer.
I want to wish you all a year of health, happiness, new knowledge and
fun,
For at the end of this week the old year is done.
May the new one be better.
May you not be a debtor.
May you grow spiritually and do much good,
And get closer and closer to sainthood.

~New Year -3

Happy Holidays to the whole staff
On the management's behalf.
Take a break, even if your work is not done.
Party and have fun!
For the new year we are wishing you all the best
Hoping that with good fortune you and your family will be
blessed!

~New Year -4

Wishing you and your family a healthy new year
Full of lots of company profits which are clear.
Thank you all for your hard work.
We are very glad that this you do not shirk.
Our profits are very important to us
So we are glad that over the amount of work that you have you do
not fuss.
Without all of you the work would not get done
And I would not be able to have fun.
Seriously I give many thanks
To everyone through the ranks.
Your work is top notch
And I hardly need my scotch.
I can really rely on all of you
Your work is professional through and through.
Let's toast a new year full of smiles
And not too many trials,
Where profits are high,
And everyone is happy with their share of the pie!

Purim

~Purim -1

On Purim people give gifts of *mishloah manot*,
And with mine I am sending this little note.
That we consider you a friend we want to explain
And over the food in the basket we hope you will not complain.
We hope that our basket does add
To your feeling this Purim of being glad.
We hope that you will feel very stable,
And that you will always have enough food to put on your table.

~Purim -2

It's Purim time once more,
And that's why you will find this food basket at your door.
We are sending you this basket of food,
Hoping that it does put you in a good mood.

~Purim -3

Once again it is Purim time,
But instead of a food basket, you are receiving this rhyme.
I have given to *the food bank a donation,
To help a **family with determination.
For what could be more worthwhile?
Than **a family with a smile!

*Write name of place that you gave donation.
**Can change to "an adult", "a child" or anything else appropriate.

~Purim -4

In lieu of *mishloah manot*,
You are being sent this little note,
As I gave a donation,
And am now sending you this explanation.
Instead of putting more food in your stockpile,
The money has gone to help *a child smile.
We hope that on this Purim you will be especially glad,
Knowing that to the quality of life of *a child at **the hospital this donation did add.

*Can substitute a person, an adult, someone, etc.
**Fill in the name of the organization donated to.

~Purim -5

Purim is a time of smiles,
When we try to forget our trials,
So we hope that this Purim you are happy and gay
And that you are healthy we do pray.
Because you are our friend
This food basket to you we do send.

~Purim -6

On Purim it is traditional to give food,
And we don't want to be rude,
But we felt that it would be more meaningful for you,
If a donation was made instead of giving you more on which to chew.
*The food bank I did choose,
Hoping that about the importance of **feeding the hungry you do share my views.

*Fill in the name of the charity.
**Fill in something about the chosen organization.

Thanksgiving

On Thanksgiving we think of turkey and pumpkin pie
And friends and neighbors who we ask to drop by.
But really it is a day,
To give thanks for everything that has come our way.

Valentine's Day

~Valentine's Day -1

You're friendship is special to me
So I hope that my valentine you will agree to be.

~Valentine's Day -2

Happy Valentine's Day to a special friend.
With you I like time to spend.
In you I know that I can confide
And that to my life you are a guide.
Good advice you do provide,
But above all you make me feel good inside.

~Valentine's Day -3

I'm sorry that I'm away
But I still wanted to wish you a happy Valentine's Day.
In distance we may not be near
But to me our friendship is still clear.

~Valentine's Day -4

Love is shown in many ways
And it is highlighted on a few special days.
Today is Valentine's and we will go out to dine
On good food and wine,
As a symbol of how much I love you
And as thanks for all that you do.
If you agree to be mine
Then I know that life will be just fine.
Without you my life would not be the same
And so, "I love you" I would like to proclaim.

IMPROVEMENT

Feel free
To write a note to me.
It can be long or short,
About something that you disagree with or support.
Thanks for taking the time
For helping to make our work place more sublime.

INVITATIONS

~Invitation -1

You we would like to invite,
For a dinner *Sunday, April 21st at night.
Some of us would like to celebrate your **anniversary of ***40 years,
To your achievement we would like to raise our glasses for a few cheers!

*Put in the day and date of the celebration.
**May write any kind of celebration (birthday, graduation after X years, working for X years, etc.)
***You can change the number of years.

~Invitation -2

For a *birthday lunch, you, we would like to invite,
Because that your *birthday is coming up we have not lost sight.
On **Sunday the 21st of this month at noon,
We would like to celebrate with you if that is opportune.

*You can change the event to an anniversary, graduation, etc.
**Write day and date.

~Invitation -3

So, you think that your *birthday slipped our mind,
But we simply decided to have a celebration of a different kind.
So although it was a surprise until now,
At this point we hope that you will say WOW!

*Can change type of celebration.

~Invitation -4

*Sunday, April 21st at the hour of nine,
Is the date and time that we did assign,
For a breakfast that is sure to be divine.

We look forward to celebrating your **birthday with you.
We are sorry that we can't arrange a picnic with a view,
But we can promise that our friendship is true.

*Write the day and date
**You can change the reason for the celebration.

~Invitation -5

A little belated it is true,
But finally we are all together and we want to celebrate your
*birthday with you.
This **Tuesday, we request your presence at **one o'clock,
At which time the door to ****your favorite restaurant you may
unlock.

*You can change the reason for the celebration
**You can change the day and time.
***Write the location where you will be meeting.

114

~Invitation -6

This is an invitation,
To an important celebration,
That we hope will meet with your expectation.

*Thursday at **eight o'clock,
Our goodies will be unlocked,
And we can begin to birthday rock!

*Write day and date.
**Write time.

~Invitation -7

What do you think about lunch at the hour of one?
Do you think that can be done?
Well, we have all agreed,
And are now waiting for your permission to proceed.
We would all like to invite you,
To celebrate the years that you did accrue.
On *Sunday the **second,
Is the best time we do reckon.
***To put our differences away,
Even if it is a little early and celebrate your special day.

*Write in day and date.
**This works for "the second" or "twenty-second".
***The last two lines can be left out if not appropriate.

~Invitation -8

Please join me at the hour of one,
For food and fun.
On *Friday, April 21st we will meet,
And I'm sure that it will be a treat.
Please join me for lunch,
Because as you know we **all like to munch.

*Write in day and date.
**Can be changed to "we both like".

~Invitation -9

On *Sunday, April 21st at **one o'clock,
To ***my house we will ask you to walk.
There we would like to celebrate with you,
Your ****birthday which we really do want to pursue.
We hope by then that hungry and excited you will be.
That we all want this to be a nice celebration for you, we do all agree!!

*Write in day and date.
**You can change the time.
***You can change the location.
****You can change the type of celebration.

~Invitation -10

At *Jill's house we will meet.
I'm sure that it will be a treat.
We're looking forward to **Bill's talk.
I'm sure that it will be well worth the walk.

*Fill in name of host/ess or write my house.
**Fill in name of speaker.

~Invitation -11

On *Sunday, February 15th to **Jill's we will go.
You really can't say no.
She makes me feel like a queen,
So to go to her house I am keen.
So get ready to put on your shoes.
You really can't lose.

*Fill in day and date
**Fill in host/ess

~Invitation -12

Please come and be my guest.
To serve a nice *lunch I will do my best.
I hope that you will all come and sit in a chair
As about each and every one of you I do care.

*You can substitute dinner, supper, brunch, breakfast.

~Invitation -13

At my house we will gather.
Nowhere else would I rather.
I will slave away,
Night and day,
And come *Sunday, April 21st I will say,
"Where is everyone today?"
So please help me out,
I don't want to pout.
Come by foot, or by car,
Come from near or far.
I'll try to make it worthwhile
And you will certainly make me smile.

*Fill in day and date.

~Invitation -14

On *Sunday, April 21st please come to my house and join me
At **2:00 for ***cookies and tea.
Together we can talk all day
And keep our minds from decay.

*Fill in the day and date.
**Fill in time.
***You can substitute a meal, add in coffee or wine, or anything else
appropriate.

~Invitation -15

We would like to invite you to a *birthday lunch,
That we hope will satisfy you so that all afternoon you won't have to
munch.
With your permission we will meet to eat and have some fun,
On **Sunday, April 21st at the hour of one.
We hope that the lunch will meet with your scrutiny,
Because we sure don't want a mutiny!!

*Can change the type of celebration.
**Put the day and date of the celebration.

~Invitation -16

On *Thursday at nine in the morning,
We are already giving you warning,
That we will be giving you a party,
That will consist of a breakfast that is hearty.

*Can change day and time.

~Invitation -17

Join us at the hour of nine,
At which time on breakfast we will dine.
On *Thursday, April 21st we will meet,
And we're sure that it will be a treat.
**My house will be the location.
We look forward to this celebration!

*Write day and date.
**Write name of location, or "We will meet you in the usual
location."

~Invitation -18

That you are a little sad we have seen
So we are putting together some nice cuisine
To celebrate your *special birthday which we hope will not be
routine.

So here is a proper note,
With a place and time that you can quote,
Because I do not want tears in your throat.

On **Sunday, April 21st please join us,
Over lunch at ***1:00 we will make a fuss,
And about this *birthday I'm sure we'll have a lot to discuss.

*Can change the reason for getting together.
**Write day and date.
***Write time.

KITCHEN AREA

Dirty Dishes in the Sink

~Dirty Dishes in the Sink -1

There were dirty dishes in the sink
And they were starting to stink.
Please wash your dishes right away
So that any food left on them does not have time to decay.

~Dirty Dishes in the Sink -2

Dirty dishes sitting around.
Oh what germs can be found!
This is a sight I rather not see.
Don't you agree?
Please keep the place clean,
So we don't need a vaccine!

Missing Food from Fridge

~Missing Food from Fridge -1

Beware! This fridge ate my food
And I think that it is very rude.
I'm warning you in advance,
You may not want to take a chance.
Keep your food and drinks far away
Or you too could be left in dismay!

~Missing Food from Fridge -2

Warning!
I could not find my food this morning.
Perhaps you saw it run away?
You called "stop" but it would not stay?
If this fridge is not acting nicely to the food,
If it is in any way being rude,
Please inform me right away,
So that I can take care of it without delay.

Using Boiling Water

If the boiling water in the kettle you finish,
Or for less than a cup it did diminish,
Please fill the kettle and turn it on once more,
As I keep filling the kettle and coming back to find that there is no
water left to pour.
Thank you for helping with this deed
So that to have a hot drink I too can succeed!

LEAVING WORK

~Leaving Work -1

Your time has come to go,
About this we are sad, we hope you know.
It's been lots of fun working with you,
There is no one else that we would have preferred on our crew.
We hope that more of you we will see,
Because to be with you is as pleasant as can be.
This present is a little token,
Hoping that all thoughts of us will not be broken.

~Leaving Work -2

We hope that at the hour of ten,
You will be ready to put down your pen.
We want to say our goodbyes
And give you a little surprise.

~Leaving Work -3

At *2:00 in your honor we are serving something to eat,
As sitting around eating and talking on your last day just can't be
beat.

*Write in the time.

~Leaving Work -4

So, today working at *the food bank is your last day,
And we will surely miss you when you are far away.
We are sure that many interesting things you will see,
But that we will miss you, we all agree.
For us you have helped to make things run smoothly without any
doubt,
But that is not what made you stand out.
Your personality, friendliness and humor,
Are far more than a rumor.
We always saw you with a smile,
And talking with you was always worthwhile.
We are truly sorry to see you go,
But we are sure with so many new experiences in **Chicago your
face will be aglow.
So be healthy,
And don't worry whether or not you are wealthy.
Enjoy yourself a lot,
But remember the rules that to you your mother taught.
Don't commit any crime,
And remember us from time to time.
We would love to receive an email from you,
To tell us of various experiences you did accrue.
We must say bye for now,
And we hope that **Chicago to you will be one big WOW!

*Fill in name of company.
**Fill in name of new place of work, or new city.

~Leaving Work -5

*You have been **Jill's loyal aide,
But more than that, true friendship have you displayed.
You have always given good advice,
But above all you are simply really nice.
It is sad that you are leaving the ***food bank team,
Your work really has been supreme.
We are relieved that at least we will see you now and then.
What would we ever do if we would not see you again?
With our wish please comply,
And every once in a while come by.

*If this is not relevant leave out the first two lines.
**Write in name of superior.
***Write in the name of the company, project or division.

~Leaving Work -6

We will miss hearing you talk to yourself.
We will miss wondering if beside you is a little elf.
We will miss your laughter.
But we will definitely remember you forever after.
We don't know what we will do without you.
Perhaps before you go you can give us a clue.

~Leaving Work -7

This plant is for you,
We really think that it is due.
We know that you didn't want anything when you went today,
But this is just a little something for you to take away.
It really was nice working with you,
And we hope that this is not *adieu*.

~Leaving Work -8

You certainly helped *the hospital gift shop along,
You helped it to become strong.
**We hope that you will have good memories of all the years,
That you have worked with not only our office, but the
customers, and the volunteers.
Well, your time has come for a whole new beginning,
And with this decision we hope that you are grinning.
There's so much that you can do now.
You can take up a new sport, or pottery, or learn to milk a cow.
With your family you can spend more time.
You can walk in nature and other things which can be sublime.
We truly wish you well in all that you decide to do,
Whether it is something you have never tried or something that
you renew.
The most important thing is to take care of yourself,
And to listen to within you to the little elf.
We all wish you the best,
In whatever your quest.

*Write in name of company or project.
**You can leave out this line and the next if not relevant.

~Leaving Work -9

So, the time has come for you to leave,
And over this we do grieve.
We weren't sure what to make you for this little brunch,
As we understand that you have very specific ideas about what
you like to munch.
We hope that this brunch meets with your approval,
And that you know that your condemnation of the cafeteria food
has nothing to do with your removal.
You will certainly be missed.
Your stories and laughter have been hard to resist.
We will really miss every morning your little story,
Of battling traffic and finding a parking spot which seem to bring
you glory.
We wish you lots of luck finding a new career,
And if you don't succeed perhaps here you will reappear.
So, the time has come to say goodbye.
We hope that to come by and say hello you won't be shy.
We wish you luck in whatever you do,
And that you find something worthwhile to pursue.

~Leaving Work -10

We are very sorry to see you go,
It was nice to have you here though.
You *weren't here that long,
But you helped to make our team strong.
It was great to get to know you better,
We hope that from time to time you will drop us an email letter.
On your new job we would like to offer you congratulations.
We hope that you fit in without any complications.
Of course the crew can't be as nice as us,
But not everything in a job can be a plus.
**We are really going to miss your curiosity,
And hope that you are not leaving with any animosity.
**With you leaving we are not sure how we will keep track of
what is going on,
For in this endeavor you were an important pawn.
We sincerely wish you all the best,
And until you begin your new job enjoy the rest!

*Can change it to, "You were here for long,
And you helped make our team strong."
**If not appropriate leave this line and the following
corresponding line out.

~Leaving Work –11

It has really been a pleasure to work with you,
You really became an integral part of our crew,
Not at all like you were just passing through.

You were really put to the test,
With you we really were impressed,
And we all agree that you now deserve a rest.

We wish you happiness in whatever you pursue,
And hope that every once in a while you'll pass through,
As your friendship we want to pursue.

~Leaving Work -12

Your time with us was short,
But you really did add a lot of support.
You entered lots of data quickly and well,
And you even *made many friends before it was time to say
farewell.
We understand that now it is time for you to move on,
But of course we wanted to say a proper goodbye before you were
gone.
This **breakfast is a little thank you from us all,
For your work and your input about ***medicine, food and
anything else that did bounce off the wall.
Of course we wish you all the best,
And may you have success in your life's quest.

*Write in anything appropriate.
**Can substitute lunch or gift.
***You can change topics listed.

~Leaving Work -13

It has been very nice having you work with us.
You have done a good job and haven't made any fuss.
You are very pleasant to have around.
We wish for your blessings to abound.
Unfortunately we can't keep you working here,
But we hope that better things for you on your horizon will
appear.

~Leaving Work -14

We're not too sure what you thought,
Before in this job you were caught.
You were always calm, cool and collected,
And for this and your work you have become well respected.
You really will be missed,
And we hope that offers come your way that you cannot resist.

~Leaving Work -15

To *Jill we will say farewell,
Even though **she has been swell.
For the time we had together we will have a little celebration.
We will meet you in the usual location.

*Fill in name of worker.
**Can be changed to "he".

~Leaving Work –16

We are so sorry that you are leaving our little team,
Working with you has been supreme.
We certainly wish you all the best,
And hope that you find health, happiness and fulfillment in your
quest.

For an Intern or Volunteer

~Intern or Volunteer -1

You have been just great!
Over this there can be no debate.
You always had a smile,
And your work was more than worthwhile.
You helped us with *media, mailings and more,
And you never acted like any of it was a chore.
We wish you all the best in whatever you decide to pursue.
To you we want to say one big thank you.

*You can change the jobs to anything appropriate.

~Intern or Volunteer -2

You helped us get out the packets with success,
And you did it all without feeling any stress!
We appreciate your folding, and preparing the packets for mail
And that you checked the letters paying attention to detail.
We wish you the best with whatever you decide to pursue,
And once again, we would like to thank you.

~Intern or Volunteer -3

It is hard to believe
That you are going to leave.
We were really pleased with your work.
Having you here for us was really a perk.

Leaving Work Temporarily

~Leaving Temporarily -1

We are sure that the *chicken here you will not really miss,
But if we didn't tell you how much we will miss you, we would
really be amiss.
You are always so cheery when you walk in,
No matter how badly the traffic got under your skin.
We really hope that only a small break this parting will be.
That you are very easy to work with we all agree.

*Write in something appropriate (lunches, some aspect of work,
coffee, etc.)

~Leaving Temporarily -2

We hope that your time off will be just great,
And that you will keep us up-to-date.
We look forward to seeing you back,
As with your work you have quite a knack.

LOST ARTICLES

~Lost Articles -1

It is just not fair,
I put my *cup down with care
And now it is not there.
And I don't even have a spare!
Oh, I am in such despair!!
I can't imagine that it vanished into thin air.
If you know anything about this affair
Perhaps with me this information you could share,
Or just replace it when I am unaware –
If not – take care!!
And beware!

*Fill in any article that goes missing such as a pen, stapler, etc.

~Lost Articles -2

My *mug is nowhere to be found
And I have looked all around.
If my *cup you did take
I'm sure that it was by mistake.
I would appreciate you bringing it back
Before I have a panic attack!

*Fill in any article that goes missing such as a pen, stapler, etc.

MEETINGS

~Meeting -1

At *2:30, in our regular spot, we will be having our meeting
And for you there will be seating.
Please come with your ideas and open mind
So that to any problems solutions we can find.

*Fill in appropriate time.

~Meeting -2

Your attendance is requested
So that we can go over some ideas that were suggested.
About these we would like to talk,
So please let me know if you can come on *April, 21st at ten
o'clock.
In my office we will meet,
To see if we can make some suggestions concrete.

*Fill in appropriate date and time.

~Meeting -3

I would like to have a meeting
And you are one of the people that I would like to be greeting.
So please let me know if at *13:30 on Monday, April 21st you can
come
So I know if for this meeting there will be a large enough sum.

*Fill in appropriate time, day and date.

~Meeting -4

I think that things are going along great
But it is time for an update.
Tomorrow let's get together and talk
In my office at *eleven o'clock.

*Fill in appropriate time.

~Meeting -5

A reminder to you I want to convey
That we have a meeting in the board room at *10:30 today.
Please do not be late
As we have a lot that we need to update.

*Fill in appropriate time.

~Meeting -6

Today, in *the staff room we will meet
Where from **3:00-4:30 our work we will complete.
Come and make your coffee or tea
And let's see on what we can agree.

*Fill in appropriate location.
**Fill in appropriate times.

NEW CAR

I see that you have a new car.
May it drive well and not do anything bizarre!

NEW HOME

~New Home -1

So your big week has come,
And we hope that with no major problems you will succumb.
Try to think of the move as a new place that you are to go,
Rather than you are moving away from what you know.
*You are getting a brand new house that is all your own.
We hope that with its homeliness you are overblown.
May your move go without too much trouble.
May all of your possessions arrive as if they floated over in a bubble.
We hope that in time any doubts of your move will disappear,
And you will sit around saluting your good decision over a beer.

*If it is not a newly built house leave out this line and the next.

~New Home -2

We hope that moving for you isn't too hard,
And that you don't find that any special things you have to discard.
Just keep thinking of your final goal,
At the end over your own new large house you will have control.

~New Home -3

We hope that your move went well,
And that your new home is already more than just a place to dwell.
We know that to move is tiring,
And that it creates a lot of perspiring.
It is simply exhausting,
And over every extra it is easy to worry what it is costing.
But we all hope that in the not too long future down the road,
You will forget the hard times and look around and say, "Wow, what
a great abode!"

~New Home -4

May you settle into your house better and faster than you planned,
And at least one of life's mysteries you should begin to understand.
May the transition between your old and new home be easy,
And living in your new house should never make you feel queasy.

~New Home -5

Good luck with your new house,
We hope that you have many special times there with your spouse.
May you celebrate many occasions there which make you smile,
And have many discussions which you feel are worthwhile.

~New Home -6

To a new apartment you are about to move,
And with this new location we hope your life does improve.

PHONE MEMO

I want you to know
The information below:
At _____ o'clock
_____ phoned to talk.

PHOTOCOPY MACHINE

~Photocopy Machine -1

If your paper should become stuck,
Please don't play with the machine hoping for some luck.
Call me
And I will get it free.

~Photocopy Machine -2

If this machine has no more ink,
Or a light does blink,
Please give me a call
And I will come down the hall.
Please don't try to fix the machine
As it may not be something routine.
I would hate for you to make things worse
As then upon you I may put a curse!

PRAYER

Dear God
Thank you very much for giving us a new day.
Please help us to use it in a good way.
Thank you for all the beauty that we see,
For the water, the flowers, the birds and each and every tree.
I will try to make this world a nice place,
And keep a smile on my face.

PRIVATE PHONE CALLS

~Private Phone Calls -1

If in the office you insist on having a private conversation
Please make it of a short duration.
Other people are trying to get their work done
And find it hard when having to listen in to see if you are having
any fun!

~Private Phone Calls -2

Please keep your voice down while you are on the phone
As in this room you are not alone.
It is hard for others to keep their concentration
While you are having a conversation.

PROPOSAL

~Proposal -1

Please agree
That your love will be only for me.
That together we will grow old
And hopefully have lots of grandchildren to hold.
Together our goals we will pursue
And memories we will accrue.
In marriage I would like to take your hand
And place upon it a wedding band.
To signify that our love should never end
That from now until eternity our lives will blend.
We will help each other with all the trials that life brings
And enjoy together the fun things.
With you by my side
I will face life with pride.
I will be able to smile each day
And face whatever comes my way.

~Proposal -2

Please agree to be mine
So that together we can hang out a "Mr. and Mrs." sign.
Yes, I am actually asking for your hand
Because with you by my side I think that life will be grand.
I pray that you will say yes,
So that together our lives can progress
As husband and wife
Supporting each other through the trials and joy of life.

RECEIVING A BONUS

Thank you for the bonus.
I know on you was the onus.
Appreciated is the work, it is nice to know,
Now forward to next *year we can go.
It is nice working with you,
Let's hope that this year goes smoothly for the whole crew.

*Can change to the next project.

REQUEST FOR FUNDRAISING

~Request -1

I am *biking from the heart,
With a message that I want to impart.
To **these children small things can be a trial,
But after much hard work we usually see a smile.
So to raise money I do aspire,
Because the work at ***the community center I do admire.

*Fill in type of activity running, cycling, swimming, reading, etc.
**Fill in something about who the money is being raised for e.g. a
child, people in need, people with handicaps, etc.
***Fill in the name of the charity.

~Request -2

The *food bank I want to tell you a little bit about.
It is a place where the staff works a lot of miracles because they are
so devout.
For these **hungry people, a ***swimming fund raiser came about.
It is one that is also a challenge to the fund raisers without a doubt.
Help these **hungry people live their lives to the fullest, I hope that
you will,
Because they have so many dreams that they would like to fulfill.
To the address below a check you may send,
And I truly hope that this year to you brings a good end.
If you prefer by credit card on the web site you may pay,
And I hope that this coming year brings you health and happiness in
every way.

*Fill in name of organization that you are raising money for.
**Can use adults, children, youth, etc.
***Fill in type of fundraiser.

~Request -3

I spend long hours raising money and training,
And this can definitely be draining.
Yet I know that the money is all for a good cause,
And for donating in my name I give you applause.
I hope that lots of money will come my way,
As I train day after day.

SPEAKING ONE'S MIND

Congratulations to you.
You saw an opening and the opportunity you did pursue.
We all think that you did the right thing,
And hope that results it does bring.
But no matter what, it laid our feelings on the table,
And we thank you for speaking up in a way that was so able.

THANK YOU

~Thank You -1

*Jill you are a really good friend,
And you help me with everything that I have to contend.
I always feel that to me you have an open door,
Because of you I can do ever so much more.
You are always there in the time of my need,
Without you I really could not succeed.
So ...for so many reasons,
I hope that together we will spend many more seasons.
All that you do for me is key.
Thank you for helping me.

*Write person's name

~Thank You -2

Thank you so much for your note,
It means so much what you wrote.

~Thank You -3

Once again we want to thank you.
You went away and brought us something new.
About us you really did not have to think,
But you did and so we are really tickled pink.

~Thank You -4

Thank you for your poem,
I read it when I got home.
It really touched my heart,
That you thought about what will be when we are apart.
So for thinking of me,
I thank you very sincerely.

~Thank You -5

I would like to thank our hostess and our host,
And to that end I would like to make a toast.
So will you all please raise your glass,
As a way of saying that we think *Bill and Jill are first class.
We thank them for putting themselves out for us,
And making over us a fuss.
The company is great and outstanding is the food.
We will all be sorry when this evening does conclude.
But as much as we would like to stay,
We will just settle for another invitation a different day.
Thank you both so very much for this dinner,
It was really a winner.

*Fill in the names of the host and hostess.

~Thank You -6

We want to thank you so much for the gift.
You really did give *our souls a lift.

*You can substitute "us" for "our souls".

~Thank You -7

Thank you so much for the basket,
Now I have a reason to sing, "A tisket a tasket".
So if you hear me humming while I walk down the hall,
You will know that my shrink you do not need to call.

~Thank You -8

To you we really want to say thank you.
Too many people say, "I no can do".
But you helped *us a lot
So thank you so much for giving more than just a thought.

*Can change to: me, the name of an organization, a family name, etc.

~Thank You -9

Thank you so very much,
The hearts of *many you did touch.
A good deed you really did do.
The number of people as good as you are too few.

*Can substitute with: "each of us", or change to "My heart you really
did touch." or "Our hearts you really did touch."

Thank You to Guests for Coming

~Thank you to Guests -1

Thank you to *Granny Smith who did agree
To come all this way to be with me.
*Aunt Jill and *Uncle Bill from **Toronto did come too.
I'm so happy to see both of you.
From **Chicago, *cousin Bob and *Amy did fly.
Thank you for not letting my ***birthday just pass by.
I love you all very much.
Thank you for coming and staying in touch.

*Fill in appropriate names.
**Fill in appropriate places.
***Fill in occasion (Bar/Bat Mitzvah, our wedding, etc.)

~Thank You to Guests -2

At a special time like this we give thanks to have you all near.
We really appreciate all your efforts to come here.

TRAVEL

Wishes for a Good Trip

~Good Trip -1

We're so glad for you that you're going on vacation,
And we know that you won't be in isolation.
For you we really are elated,
As we know that for this trip you have waited.
We're not quite sure how we will manage without you.
Perhaps over all the tasks you perform we should review.
But much sadder is the fact,
That we will miss the way that with us you do interact.
We will really miss you,
But we're so happy for you that we just can't be blue.

~Good Trip -2

So, you're going off again in a jeep,
And this time it is even relatively cheap.
Over everyday problems don't even give a thought.
Just enjoy yourself a lot.

~Good Trip -3

So, you're off with your wife and kids – all three,
And that you will have a great time we can almost guarantee.
We're sure that your kids will enjoy the airplane flights,
And we hope that you see some great sights.
We are interested to see your pictures after your trip,
So pack your camera and opportunities to photograph don't skip.
For your kids this will be a real education.
Just forget about us and enjoy your vacation!!

~Good Trip -4

*Ontario you picked as your destination,
To take your family on vacation.
We hope that you have a great time relaxing and hiking,
And that everything is to your liking.
Let your worries be none.
Just go and have lots of fun!

*Write in the travel destination.

~Good Trip -5

We really do wonder where you will think to travel to next,
You can be sure that we are all perplexed.
We think that we should have a contest,
But you can be sure that we wish you all the best.

~Good Trip -6

We all hope that you have a great time,
And that you are not the victim of any crime.
While you are away don't worry about us,
We'll just be here slaving away, not making a fuss.

~Good Trip -7

We're happy that with family you will be,
Although we are sorry that from our lives you will be absentee.
We hope that you will see something new and have a rest,
As here you answer our every request.
Enjoy your vacation,
We're sure that to be with your family will be a great sensation.
We will try to manage without you,
After all, perhaps the time for us to learn a thing or two is overdue.

~Good Trip -8

We hope that you have a great trip,
And that you get to where you want without having to bite your lip.
We hope that you have a great time,
And that there are moments that are truly sublime.
We can't wait about your adventures to hear,
And see your pictures which we hope come out clear.

~Good Trip -9

We're sorry to your *father you have to go,
But this trip is another opportunity to show that from you love does flow.
We know that the trip will not be an easy one,
But we hope that you will feel that it was worthwhile when it is done.
We will be thinking of you,
But of us a thought do not pursue.

*Can change the relation (friend, mother, sister, brother, etc.)

~Good Trip -10

So, your *in-laws you are going to see,
And that you deserve the vacation we all agree.
We hope that your **in-laws' celebration will be great.
For sure they will appreciate seeing you and ***Bill at any rate.
We know that a lot of time you will be traveling by car and by plane,
But we hope that a lot of quality time with ***Bill you will gain.

*Can change to any relation or the name of a city.
**Can change relation or can take out this line and the next.
***Write in spouse's name or leave out "and Bill" in this line and
"with Bill" in the last line.

~Good Trip -11

We know that this trip is not all fun,
But we hope that you will feel that it is worthwhile when it is done.
We will miss you here,
Without you it will seem queer.
We hope that you will have some sunshine,
And that you will drink some good wine.
Make good use of your time.
When you come back there will be for you a rhyme.

~Good Trip -12

Have a great time on your well-deserved vacation,
Off to another great exotic location.
As you travel and see and do amazing things we will all wait,
To see the fascinating album that we know you will create.

~Good Trip -13

We're so sad that you're leaving,
But we know that a lot of new things you will be perceiving.
We're happy for you,
And hope that a lot of new memories you will accrue.
We're sure you'll have a great trip,
And we hope that *your research gave you at least one good tip.
About us don't have a care,
Even though without you we will be in despair.
Somehow we will manage to get along,
Although without you we will not be as strong.

*Can substitute the name of someone who gave advice about what to do on the trip.

~Good Trip -14

I hope that you don't mind a short rhyme.
Right now I am really short of time.
I hope that your vacation will be great.
For your stories and pictures I await.

~Good Trip -15

We're glad for you that you are going off on another trip.
On life you truly have a firm grip.
We can't wait to hear about the *nature that you find,
Your tales and stories actually help us all to unwind.
So take everything in and enjoy the view,
The adventure, the food, the wine and the company too!

*You can substitute museums, sites, attractions, restaurants, beaches,
etc.

~Good Trip -16

We are sure that you will have a great trip,
But we do want to give you one tip.
About all of us and the office just forget,
This is one trip that for sure you will not regret!

~Good Trip -17

From work you may only be taking off one day,
But we are so glad that you are getting away.
You're sure to feel more refreshed when you come back,
And we'll be glad to hear about your weekend over a snack.

~Good Trip -18

It is hard to write you another rhyme,
As you keep leaving us all the time.
But we do wish you a good trip, as always we do,
We can't wait to hear your stories, and your pictures to view.
We'll try to keep the office going,
Though without you it is hard to keep things flowing.
You will really be missed,
We enjoy having you in our midst.

~Good Trip -19

So, you are flying off once again.
We know by now that from traveling you cannot refrain.
We hope that some new things you will see.
That we will miss you we can almost guarantee.
Enjoy your time away from work.
We know that at times we can drive you a little berserk.

~Good Trip -20

Down south you and *Jill are to go.
When you come back we are sure that your skin will glow.
Have fun **snorkeling and bathing in the sun,
It is very important to have time together and have some fun.
Don't think of us at all,
"Office" is a word that you need not recall.
But we will truly think of you,
Because you are terrific – and that is true.

*Write in name of travelling partner or "your family".
**You can take out "snorkeling and" if it is not relevant.

~Good Trip -21

With your *brother we hope that you have a meaningful time,
Because not to spend time with a sibling is almost a crime.
So about the office don't give a thought,
Over new and old memories with your family we hope that your
mind is caught.

*Can change to sister.

~Good Trip -22

So, you're going on a trip to see the flowers,
And we hope that it gives you more powers.
We know that you will find nice places along the way to have a
snack,
And for sure more refreshed, you will come back.
Lots of colorful pictures we know that you will take,
And we look forward to seeing them while taking a break.
Of course we will miss talking to you,
But we are happy knowing that the important things in life you do
pursue.
Like being with your husband, and looking at each flower,
And of course eating sandwiches every hour.

Welcome Back

~Welcome Back -1

You were really missed,
But we know that this vacation you couldn't resist.
We're sure that stories you will have to tell,
Because with *your grandchildren you did dwell.
About all of your adventures we can't wait to hear,
So start talking as you now have our collective ear.

*Fill in appropriate name or names.

~Welcome Back -2

We are so glad to have you back.
Without you we really did feel a lack.
From your travels we want to hear lots of stories,
And from your bags we want to take inventories.
To see your pictures will be a treat,
But most of all we want to see your face because it is so sweet.
We're happy that you had such a good time,
And of course we hope you like your welcome back rhyme.

~Welcome Back -3

You must have so much to tell,
So many things you have seen since to us you said farewell.
We're happy for you that you got away,
And want to hear the details of what you did day by day.
We know that of your trip we can only really get a small taste,
But we're sure that your memories cannot be replaced.

~Welcome Back -4

Welcome back to the land of reality,
Where we are waiting to hear about your adventures in totality!

~Welcome Back -5

Welcome back.
We really felt a lack.
When you were away we were quite sad.
To have you back we are very glad!

~Welcome Back -6

We're sure that you have stories to tell,
But most of all we hope that your *mom is well.
Hopefully a few pictures you did take,
And of interesting outings you did partake.

*Can change to any type of relative or name.

~Welcome Back -7

Welcome back to Grandma number one,
We are sure that your grandchildren lacked none.
You all, for sure, saw many terrific things,
And we're sure that your grandchildren felt like kings.

~Welcome Back -8

Now it is time to get back to real life,
Going to the office, and going home and being just man and wife.

~Welcome Back -9

We hope that you had a good change,
And that on your money you got a good exchange.
We figure that now you are ready to go,
To strive towards some new plateau.

~Welcome Back -10

Welcome back from your vacation.
We hope that you had a lot of relaxation.
About your trip we can't wait to hear.
We certainly hope that you created memories that will not disappear.

~Welcome Back -11

From your holiday we welcome you back.
We hope that returning to reality does not give you a panic attack.

~Welcome Back -12

You were certainly missed around here.
We kept hoping that you would just reappear.
But for good things we are told, you have to wait,
So we waited and waited and finally today reappears our soul mate.
We're so glad that you're back,
Especially because we had to pick up your slack.
We were glad to get emails and know that things were going well,
But now we can't wait to hear the stories that you have to tell.

~Welcome Back -13

We hope that your weekend together was just great,
And that together new memories you did create.
On a selfish note we want to say,
That we are glad that long you did not stay away.

~Welcome Back -14

From your holiday we want to welcome you back.
We hope that on your holiday rest you did not lack.
We know for sure that you had lots of sun.
We hope that you also had fun!

~Welcome Back -15

We hope that your trip was first rate,
And that your kids behaved really great.
We hope that it was special being all together,
And that you weren't stopped doing anything because of the weather.
Of course we hope that everyone had fun,
And it would be nice if each of you felt that you were treated as
"number one".

~Welcome Back -16

We hope that while you were away of good times you did partake,
And that you had a good break.
A lot has happened while you were away,
But at least things are not in disarray.

~Welcome Back -17

Welcome back!
We hope that it was not too hard to pack.
Hopefully some good memories ran through your mind,
And you had some time to unwind.

~Welcome Back -18

We hope that the *temples were well worth seeing,
And that you are now content to keep your feet on the ground for
the time being.
We know that it was very humid and hot,
But we hope that you really did get to see a lot.

*Can substitute museums, sites, castles, etc.

~Welcome Back -19

We are especially glad to have you back from this trip well.
We're sure that you will have stories to tell.
Perhaps on this trip you gained a new perspective on life.
At any rate, we hope that you do not meet with any great strife.
It is good to have you back safe and sound.
It is always good to have you around!

~Welcome Back -20

Again from *India we welcome you back.
We hope that getting back to "real life" doesn't give you a whack.
Of your travels we can't wait to hear,
And at your picture album we would like to peer.
Of course, though, the best part of you being back,
Is that we can joke and talk over a snack.

*Can substitute any place name, or you can write, "We welcome you
back,"

~Welcome Back -21

You keep going away and coming back,
Does this mean that without us you feel a little lack?
Really it is nice having you back in your chair,
Even though we know that you get up wondering here and there.
But, we can't wait to hear about your trip,
And of course your pictures we do not want to skip.
So settle in for at least a few weeks,
Before you go traipsing off to more valleys or peaks.

~Welcome Back -22

That yesterday you came back to no poem I really do feel bad,
And I hope that you are not mad.
We're all so glad that you had a good time,
I hope that it was not marred by coming back to no rhyme.
I guess that I need you here to keep me on my toes,
Because it seems that sometimes I doze.

~Welcome Back -23

I certainly hope that you had fun.
This was certainly a great way for the New Year to have begun.
Hopefully you had a special time,
And you understand I have a lot of work so you're getting a short
rhyme.

~Welcome Back -24

We're sure you have some great pictures that you can use for a screen
saver,
And that eating outdoors gave your sandwiches a better flavor.
We're glad that you're back,
Because among other things you make more enjoyable our morning
snack.

~Welcome Back -25

Welcome back to reality,
We hope that your vacation added to your life some vitality.
That you enjoyed *the snorkeling, the sun and the sand,
And that everything was simply grand!!

*You can take out snorkeling if it is not relevant.

WEDDING

~Wedding -1

May you help each other with any fear,
So that they just disappear.
May you be thankful for the things that you accrue,
And not feel lacking for anything that does not belong to you.
May you both be well in body and mind,
And grow together and be an example to mankind.

~Wedding -2

Now you begin your life,
As husband and wife.
May your future together be full of much pleasure.
Each other may you truly treasure.
Forward in life the two of you should walk side by side.
In each other you should feel free to confide,
Advice one to the other you should gently provide.
To reach new heights the other you can guide.
In each other may you always feel pride.
Little differences may you be able to set aside.
Together, many endeavors may you pursue.
May a long and happy life unfold for you two.

~Wedding -3

*Jill and *Bill you have just begun together a new life,
As husband and wife.
**During the wedding you felt a special kind of joy.
Keep that tucked away and don't let it be destroyed.
We hope that you will have much to be thankful for,
As together the world you explore.
***But don't forget to be thankful also for the little things,
As they also were created by the King of Kings.
May you together find success and may you be blessed,
In your life's quest.
May your lives be guided by giving thanks,
And not for what is held for you in the banks.
Thank each other for things large and small,
For things that are done, and not just what is bought at the mall.
***Think of your success
As if it is from God a caress.
Help each other be strong
And know that together you belong.

*Fill in names of bride and groom.
**Can be changed to "Under the huppa" or "On the altar".
***You can leave these lines out (with their corresponding couplet) if
you don't want any reference to God.

~Wedding -4

Life is a bit like a theatrical show,
You can plan and rehearse, but you are never sure how it will go.
So take each other by the hand,
Knowing that not everything will happen just as you plan.
It is important to learn to go with the flow,
And to help each other grow.
Flowers and candy go a long way,
But affection, attention and support create feelings that stay.
So with lots of love become husband and wife,
And start together a wonderful life!

~Wedding -5

From the *food bank staff where **Jill does work,
***Bill, we can tell you that having **Jill as a ****mother-in-law is
really a perk.
To the two of you we wish a very happy life,
Together in health and fulfillment as husband and wife.

*Fill in name of company or project.
**Fill in name of worker.
***Fill in name of bride or groom marrying into the family.
****Can change to father-in-law, sister-in-law, brother-in-law, etc.

~Wedding -6

Together you have just begun what we hope will be a wonderful life,
As husband and wife.
About love I probably don't know very much,
But it seems to me that it is analogous to a gentle touch.
You know that the partner is there,
You feel them and know that they care.
Helping the other to grow,
Sometimes helping to speed things up and sometimes to take things slow.
Helping you see and face everything in your life,
And helping you minimize any potential strife.
Forward in life the two of you should walk side by side.
In each other you should feel free to confide.
Advice one to the other you should gently provide.
Little differences put aside,
But major decisions together decide.
In each other may you always feel pride!
May your future together be full of much pleasure,
And may you always realize that in each other you have a real treasure.
Together, many adventures may you have the chance to pursue,
And may a long and happy life unfold for the two of you.
May you always feel that each day with the other is the best,
And may your union be blessed!

~Wedding -7

May your marriage be blessed.
May you help each other through life's quest.
And in whatever you each endeavor
The important thing is to remain best friends forever!

~Wedding -8

Together enjoy life,
Trying to avoid strife.
Don't forget the love you felt walking down the aisle,
And always try to make each other smile.
To the other's needs attend.
Be each other's best friend.
There is not always a right and a wrong,
So compromise to get along.

~Wedding -9

Bill's office staff wishes you both all the best
And pray that your marriage will be blessed.
May you both be healthy
And realize that there are more important things than being wealthy.

May you keep the special glow
That upon you both at your wedding did show
And together may your happiness only grow.

To a Bride

For the prettiest bride that we ever did see,
You have no idea how we pray that happy you will be.
We pray that this year will be a special one for you,
As you start upon a path that is so new.
Know that as all new paths have ups and downs,
We hope that at a minimum are your frowns.
We want so much for you to show your beautiful smile.
It is something that will never go out of style.

To the Parents of the Bride or Groom

Enjoy every detail regarding the wedding,
And that your family keeps spreading.
May this year hold lots of fun, happy times and good food,
With everyone that your family does include.

WELCOME BACK AFTER MATERNITY LEAVE

~Maternity Leave -1

Welcome back!
We hope that it won't be too hard for you to get back on track.
May you easily get your work done,
So that you can go home to your son!
We know of *Billy you are probably thinking,
But don't worry, his bottle he is probably happily drinking.
We're sure that this year will be for you very sweet,
As you watch *Billy crawl and gradually stand on his feet.
May you and your family have a healthy year,
With many exciting firsts to cheer!

*Write in name of baby.

~Maternity Leave -2

We're sure that you still want to stay home and cuddle your little one,
But we're glad to have you back as work still has to get done.
It was hard without you when you were away,
So we're really glad that you came back today.

~Maternity Leave -3

It's great to see you back in your chair.
And I'm glad that you found good child care.
Let's sit down at *10:00 today
And I'll fill you in on what has been going on while you were away.

*You may change the time.

WELCOMING SOMEONE TO WORK

~Welcome -1

Welcome to our team.
We are sure that you will be supreme.
It will be, we are sure, pleasant having you around,
We are always here to help, so you don't have to feel weighed down.

~Welcome -2

Welcome to the *community center team.
You are already starting to fit in it does seem.
Know that questions you don't have to suppress,
And that we wish you much success.
We hope you will like working with us.
We're sure that to the team you will be a big plus.

*Write in name of company or project.

~Welcome -3

We really like that you will now be part of the staff.
We feel good that with you we can laugh.

~Welcome -4

To the *computer team we would like to welcome you.
We hear that you are the one to take *the division to heights that are
new.
For your projects we wish much success.
We are sure that us you will impress.

*Write the name of the company, project, or department.

~Welcome -5

To this job we would like to welcome you,
We are happy to share the knowledge that we did accrue,
And we are sure that you will be adding a new idea, or two.

We look forward to see how the *department will grow,
We're sure that your ideas will shortly begin to show,
Before long you will be leading us away from the status quo.

We wish you much success,
We hope that you will not be under too much stress,
And that your ideas get us into the press.

*Can substitute project, company, etc.

~Welcome –6

Welcome to our team,
You will help make come true our dream.
Lots of money should touch your hands,
As our work does expand to many lands.
We hope that you understand that your work in this place,
Helps put a smile on many a face.

~Welcome –7

Welcome to the team.
From what we've heard you will be supreme.
May you have an easy transition
Into your new position.
If you need help with any task,
To any of us feel free to ask.
We hope that you find this job to be ideal.
And may you have the strength to tackle it with zeal.

~Welcome –8

An official welcome we would like to send to you.
A good working relationship we certainly expect to pursue.
Any question you can ask us without hesitation,
Whether about a report, an email or a *donation.
Thank goodness for telephone calls and emails,
We're sure that we will always be able to work out any details.
We're sure that we will get along just fine,
**It's just too bad that we can't sit down over a glass of wine.

*Can change to foundation, location, rotation, corporation, computation.
**Can change to "Now let's make arrangements to sit down over a glass of wine."

WISHING SOMEONE WELL IN THEIR NEW JOB

In a new job you are about to get started,
And we're sure that you will do it full hearted.
*We will really miss you here at home,
But we know that you also need time to roam.
We are sure that you will do a good job,
And not just sit around like a blob.
Your co-workers will benefit from your work,
And we hope that you feel a perk.
In your new job we wish you good luck,
And hope that you make a decent buck.

*Take out this line and the next if not appropriate.

ABOUT THE AUTHOR

Marcia Goldlist was born in Toronto, Canada. She has a Masters of Education from the University of Toronto. In 2000 she moved to Israel with her husband and 4 daughters. She is currently the mother-in-law to three and happy grandmother to three adorable grandsons!

Marcia began by writing in rhyme for family events. She has written for special occasions such as the engagements and weddings of her daughters and the birth of a grandson when her rhymes were read in front of guests. At work Marcia started writing rhymes for staff birthdays, office memos, to disseminate information, to welcome new staff and to say goodbye to the old. As a result of this she was asked to write for other people's personal and family occasions.

The compliments and encouragement that Marcia received encouraged her to put her poetry into books so that others could also make special occasions fun and meaningful.

More rhyming books by Marcia Goldlist:
~Birthday Cards & Toasts:
Express Yourself in Rhyme
~Cards & Toasts For Almost All Occasions:
Express Yourself in Rhyme
~Cards, Toasts & Notes for the Office:
Express Yourself in Rhyme
~Enjoying Genesis: The Bible in Rhyme
~Enjoying Genesis: The Bible in Rhyme in Large Print

If you enjoyed this book look for Marcia's upcoming books:
~Enjoying Exodus: The Bible in Rhyme
~Enjoying Exodus: The Bible in Rhyme in Large Print

Visit Marcia's blog Enjoying the Bible Online for discussion points and projects related to the Bible. You can visit the blog at: http://enjoyingthebible.wordpress.com.